Pedogate Primer:
the politics of pedophilia

Philip Fairbanks

Copyright ©2020 Philip Fairbanks & Is It Wet Yet Press
All rights reserved.

No part of this book may be reproduced, or stored in a retrieval system, or transmitted in any form or by any means, electronic, mechanical, photocopying, recording, or otherwise, without express written permission of the author or publisher.

This book is dedicated to Uncle Charlie, Cousin Cyril and Athena Snows who helped me believe in myself even when I wasn't able to myself. Also dedicated to the memory of Dave McGowan the author of Programmed to Kill which is heavily cited here. Many thanks are also owed to my family and friends who always loved and supported me even when they thought I might be crazy. A huge outpouring of support and some incredible insights and tips came from the online community gathered around the work of Dave McGowan as well. Without authors like McGowan, Stephen Singular, Nick

Bryant and others who bravely covered the topic of elite and institutional pedophilia, despite the virtual media blackout, this book likely would never exist.

In addition I'd like to thank friends, family and my very supportive coworkers and bosses for pushing me to finally complete a book length work, I also appreciate everyone who agreed to be a beta reader. And of course I thank God who has brought me through the dark days and the bright and made me strong enough, tenacious enough and dogged enough to keep going against all odds regardless of what tests life handed me.

Contents

INTRODUCTION	1
BARRIE, CARROLL & HUYSMANS: Pedophilia hiding in plain view in the Victorian era	5
THE CIA's MK-Ultra EXPERIMENTS AND TRAUMA TRAINING	17
FALSE MEMORY SYNDROME FOUNDATION	23
THE FINDERS	31
Franklin Scandal	39
ABUSE OF THE CLOTH	51
CHILD ABUSE AND CULTS	61
SATANIC PANIC: McMartin and Presidio	73
HOLLYWOOD, POP CULTURE AND THE CULTURED PEDOPHILES	81
JON BENET RAMSEY	109
Beast Of Belgium: Child Exploitation And Cover-Up In The Marc Dutroux Affair	115
7th FLOOR GROUP COVER-UP	123
HARRY HAY & THE SAFE SCHOOLS	127
INSTITUTIONAL PEDOPHILIA AND GROOMING EPIDEMIC IN THE UNITED KINGDOM	135
THE JEFFREY EPSTEIN AFFAIR	143
A DIGITAL PLAYGROUND FOR PEDOPHILES	151
EPILOGUE: The Cuties Controversy	173
BIBLIOGRAPHY	187

INTRODUCTION

I've heard in the media that attempting to raise awareness about the sort of topics you'll see discussed in this book make me a potentially dangerous conspiracy theorist. Perhaps even an ideological extremist. I don't consider myself to be all that extreme personally, but what do I know about myself that the mainstream media doesn't know better?

I have been tracking some of these topics for years since I learned about the abuse of unwitting citizens, sometimes children or other vulnerable populations, being used and abused in the CIA's MK-Ultra mind control research program. MK-Ultra research led me to The Finders, the cult with a surprising intelligence community connection, that skated on child abuse charges despite evidence of international trafficking and abuse of children. Luckily for the Finders, the CIA closed the investigation when it became a federal case thanks to a Customs agent acting on tips from Tallahassee Police Department. No one was charged and the children were returned to the group.

Cults, mind control experimentation, and institutional pedophilia are topics that have obsessed me for years. It's a dark rabbit hole that most people don't care enough... or care *too much* to be able to follow too far through.

Despite the many people for decades who cry moral panic at any mention of these hot button issues, several researchers are convinced of the real danger that exists. In *Celebrity, Pedophilia, and Ideology in American Culture* author Jason Lee says:

"Despite methodological and definitional problems, many of the most respected researchers in the field claim child sexual abuse is not merely something on the fringes of society that can be put down to hysteria and media hype. For sociologist Brian Corby, children are 'subjected to far more sexual abuse than was previously imagined possible.'"

In the past few months, the situation has been ramping up to paint anyone who rails against these endemic and ever-present abuses as either a potentially dangerous domestic terrorist or, worse, in my opinion, a callous profiteer cashing in on the situation. Just in the last few weeks, Facebook has been deleting groups and suppressing hashtags such as Pedogate, #savethechildren, #saveourchildren, and similarly related terms. This does not dissuade me, rather it further convinces me of the importance of covering these topics.

I find it astounding that with the Jeffrey Epstein story having finally made news that the idea of widespread pedophile networks, some including people in positions of power or very high places, seems so hard to believe. I was writing about Epstein and social media and YouTube grooming for years before the *New York Times* and others finally decided the story was too big to ignore anymore. I received no awards or commendations and am not seeking them now. I aim to share information about a sensitive topic that is easy to hide because so many people would rather *not* believe, would rather *not* see.

Researcher Dave McGowan coined the term "The Pedophocracy" to describe a system of power held and kept in place through ritual child abuse as a means of entrapment and blackmail. Like the idea that certain members of the government plan false-flag terror attacks the very premise is so disturbing, that most people will reject it on the surface without even taking the time to examine any evidence of its veracity. Even Israeli paper *Ha'aretz* admits the existence of the USS Liberty false flag. The Gulf of Tonkin incident that precipitated the Vietnam war is another example. Some things just seem too horrible to be true. Unfortunately, that doesn't make them untrue.

Transpersonal Psychologist Dr. Charles Tart describes the condition of consensus trance as a situation where, even while awake, humans wander through life somewhat as if it were a dream. In the early 2000's I briefly corresponded with Dr. Tart, even called for a conversation. Dr. Tart's thesis proposes the idea that we are something like sleepwalkers and see what we are conditioned to see, what we expect to see. If this is so, likely it cuts both ways. Meaning, we are even more likely to not see what we don't expect to see, what is too horrific to envision. And what could be more horrific than the idea that many people at the upper echelons of society, charity and aid organizations, churches, and of course the movers, shakers, and power brokers, are either directly involved in, or at least complicit in, the wholesale abuse of children?

Bear in mind, this book is, as it purports to be, simply a primer. I'm just scratching the surface here. I wish I had time to get further into the growing MAP (minor-attracted persons) community on Twitter, the VirPed (virtuous pedophile) terminology being thrown around in the community, and several other subjects. The connection between pedophilia and serial killer phenomena is also a fascinating topic as are the allegations that Charles Manson was a child trafficker. I also could have expanded on the section on Hollywood pedophilia by including such films as Brooke Shield's *Pretty Baby* and other highly regarded movies that feature eroticized nude children. If I were to cover every facet, this tome would expand to several volumes and after months of spending several hours a day delving into these dark depths, I'm already having sleep disturbances and nightmares. Hopefully, this somewhat short volume will be at least a sufficient jumping off point into further research for interested individuals.

Dave McGowan's *Programmed to Kill* was a vital inspiration for this book. I highly encourage anyone looking to learn more to seek out a copy. It's a horrific and fact-filled page-turner but, if you're like me, you may need to take a few days break in between sections. Perhaps the same advice would apply to this book. Nick Bryant's exhaustively documented book *The Franklin Scandal: A Story of Powerbrokers, Child Abuse and Betrayal* is another vital volume for those interested in further reading that is also perhaps best handled small doses at a time.

Lastly, I want to say remember that despite the darkness in the world, there is still light, and as bad as it seems, as bad as it is, there is still goodness in the world. The tiniest of lights eliminate the existence of absolute darkness.

BARRIE, CARROLL & HUYSMANS:
Pedophilia hiding in plain view in the Victorian era

Two of the most famous, beloved, and enduring of all children's stories are *Peter Pan* and *Alice's Adventures in Wonderland* and of course its companion *Through the Looking Glass*. Lesser known are the claims that the authors may have had an unhealthy preoccupation with children. Perhaps even verging on or entering into the realm of pedophilia.

"May God blast anyone who writes a biography of me," read J.M. Barrie's curse in one of his last notebooks.

Justine Picardie author of the novel *Daphne* about Daphne du Maurier did extensive research on the du Maurier family which entailed learning quite a bit about Barrie whose story is so inextricably bound to theirs. She alludes to a caution verging on superstition related to that curse.

Piers Dudgeon's book *Captivated: The Dark Side of Never Never Land* makes some bold claims including that Barrie was something of a Svengali figure in the life of the du Maurier family. Ironic considering George du Maurier was the author of *Trilby*, the book from which that term originates. Barrie was certainly entranced with mesmerism, the early art of hypnosis, according to Dudgeon's dark interpretation of the evidence. This is especially sinister considering Dudgeon's claims that Barrie insinuated himself amongst the Llewelyn Davies family becoming close to the boys and their mother before their mother and father died.

As contemporary author D.H. Lawrence put it, "J.M. Barrie has a fatal touch for those he loves. They die."

Picardie wrote the following in UK's *Telegraph*:

"It's an imaginative theory, which draws on some circumstantial evidence in Daphne du Maurier's own writing (including her macabre short stories, which Dudgeon reads as revealing Barrie's crimes), and will be of interest to anyone, like me, who has followed the twists of the du Maurier family history. Indeed, Kits Browning, Daphne's son, declares Dudgeon's book to be 'absolutely fascinating, though somewhat alarming about the extent of Barrie's sinister influence on my family.'"

Picardie seems to disavow the idea of Barrie being a pedophile. The daughter of Nico, one of the original lost boys quotes her father as saying that "of course Barrie was a lover of childhood, but was not in any sexual sense the paedophile that some claim him to have been."

Nico's daughter Laura Duguid does admit understanding why the theories about Barrie seem to have grown over the years:

"There are passages in Barrie's writing that induce a sense of unease. 'I'm certain that there was nothing paedophiliac about him,' she says, 'but he did write some creepy things in The Little White Bird.' She is referring to Barrie's novel, which contains the original story of Peter Pan, while also apparently chronicling his relationship with the young George Llewelyn Davies, for whom Barrie had invented Peter Pan."

Captain W was a thinly-veiled stand-in for Barrie, right down to being a writer with an affinity for large dogs. Picardie writes:

"George is transformed into David (the name of Barrie's dead brother), while his fictional mother, Mary (the name of Barrie's wife), is closely modeled on Sylvia. Meanwhile, the Captain seeks to assuage his thwarted paternal yearnings by winning the boy for himself: 'It was a scheme conceived in a flash, and ever since relentlessly pursued – to burrow under Mary's influence with the boy, expose her to him in all her vagaries, take him utterly from her.' Mary, however, remains 'culpably obtuse to my sinister design.' All of which may give some insight into why Barrie's original title for the story of Peter Pan was 'The Boy Who Hated Mothers.'"

This proto-Peter Pan story contains several passages that would certainly alarm those with modern sensibilities:

"David and I had a tremendous adventure. It was this – he passed the night with me... I took [his boots] off with all the coolness of an old hand, and then I placed him on my knee and removed his blouse. This was a delightful experience, but I think I remained wonderfully calm until I came somewhat too suddenly to his little braces, which agitated me profoundly... I cannot proceed in public with the disrobing of David."

Later in the story, David climbs into bed with Captain W.

"For the rest of the night he lay on me and across me, and sometimes his feet were at the bottom of the bed and sometimes on the pillow, but he always retained possession of my finger..." Meanwhile, the adult lies awake, thinking of "this little boy, who in the midst of his play while I undressed him, had suddenly buried his head on my knee" and of his "dripping little form in the bath, and how when I essayed to catch him he had slipped from my arms like a trout."

James Harding, a biographer of Gerald du Maurier admitted being uncomfortable with the scene, but defends Barrie saying:

"No writer today would publish such an account without inviting accusations of paedophilia or worse. Yet Barrie, in the manner of Lewis Carroll and his nude photographs of little girls, was consciously innocent.

His snapshots of the tiny lads frolicking bare-bottomed on the beach, the cowboy and Indian adventures he made up for them... were a means to enjoy the pleasures of fatherhood with none of the pains."

Picardie, after reading Dudgeon's work, going back to Andrew Birkin's account and going over her notes from the du Maurier archive and other sources "remain[s] uncertain about J.M. Barrie, whose chief aim seemed to be not to corrupt boys into adult desire, but for himself to rejoin them in the innocence of eternal boyhood, a Neverland where children fly away from their mothers and no one need grow old."

Not surprising that Michael Jackson would name the private theme park he invited his young boy-friends to play at bore the name Neverland Ranch. Another odd bit that Picardie mentions in her writepup at the *Telegraph* raises a few alarm bells. To Michael just before his eighth birthday:

"I wish I could be with you and your candles. You can look on me as one of your candles, the one that burns badly -- the greasy one that is bent in the middle. But still, hurray, I am Michael's candle. I wish I could see you putting on the redskin's clothes for the first time... Dear Michael, I am very fond of you, but don't tell anybody."

That was from one of the few letters that survived after Peter Llewelyn Davies destroyed the majority of Barrie's correspondence with Michael before committing suicide.

Before her death, Sylvia Llewelyn Davies left a handwritten document, which said: "What I wd like wd be if Jenny wd come to Mary & that the two together wd be looking after the boys & the house." Mary was the boys' long-standing nanny whom Sylvia trusted above all others and Jenny was Mary's sister.

But after the will was found, Barrie transcribed it himself and sent it to the boys' maternal grandmother, changing Jenny to Jimmy, so it appeared that Sylvia wished him to become the boys' guardian. Birkin observed that the "transcription was no doubt unintentional"; Dudgeon meanwhile saw the alteration as an indication that "Barrie's strategy was predatory."

"Whatever the reason," Picardie writes, "the boys became Barrie's own."

Peter wrote in 1946 of the whole affair, speaking of how he and his brothers were "spirited away, as children, from my mother's and father's friends... the whole business, as I look back on it, was almost unbelievably queer and pathetic and ludicrous and even macabre in a kind of way..." Despite all that he appeared to continue to respect Barrie and appreciate the world-famous story that bore his namesake which he referred to as "that terrible masterpiece."

"I don't believe that Uncle Jim ever experienced what one might call 'a stirring in the undergrowth' for anyone — man, woman, or child," he stated in the 1970s. On another occasion, he wrote, "All I can say is that I, who lived with him off and on for more than 20 years: who lived alone with him in his flat for five of these years: never heard one word or saw one glimmer of anything approaching homosexuality or paedophiliacy [sic] — had he had either of these leanings in however slight a symptom I would have been aware. He was an innocent — which is why he could write Peter Pan!"

Robert Boothby, a closeted bisexual friend of Nicholas (Nico) Llewelyn Davies suspected Michael, one of the lost boys as possibly being gay. He also referred to the relationship Barrie had with Michael as being "morbid" and "unhealthy." Despite all this, only circumstantial evidence exists to suggest Barrie was a pedophile, or at least that he was anything but asexual for that matter. His marriage to his wife likely ended due to "impotency."

The book *Changing the Victorian Subject* from University of Adelaide Press contains a chapter "From 'Peter Panic' to proto-Modernism: the case of J.M. Barrie." The authors, Maggie Tonkin, Mandy Treagus, Madeleine Seys, and Sharon Crozier-De Rosa take the position that any claims about Barrie are "largely based on unsubstantiated speculation and moral panic."

Carroll, though increasingly so suggested as having been a pedophile, like Barrie and Nabokov is suspected not to have acted upon it apart from his habit of taking pictures of little girls either nude or in various states of undress. Nude photography of children was not uncommon in the Victorian era, but *Artnet* reports of a particular photograph that shocked BBC documentarians during their research. A photo "no parent would have consented to" of Lorina Liddell, a sister of Alice Liddell of Alice's Adventure's fame.

Another book by an author around whom rumors of pedophilia swirl is *Lolita* by Vladimir Nabokov. Regardless of their sexual desires, Barrie, Carroll, and Nabokov's works have become iconic among self-proclaimed "childlovers" and "minor-attracted persons" as many pedophiles prefer to refer to themselves. Humbert Humbert, the protagonist in the novel *Lolita*, is the classic literary portrayal of a pedophile. Evidence is presented that the author of Lolita, Vladimir

Nabokov, was himself consciously a pedophile who "acted out his desires vicariously through his writing. Drawing upon his literary works and biography, the manifest and genetic origins of Nabokov's pedophilia are traced back to an unresolved oedipal conflict complicated by childhood sexual abuse. The raw power of Lolita derives from the abreactive discharge of a libidinal cathexis denied any other mode of expression."

Nabokov, by the way, was also an early translator of Lewis Carroll's *Alice in Wonderland* into Russian. Like J.M. Barrie's *Peter Pan* or *Alice's Adventures in Wonderland,* the themes seem to have attracted a good deal of pedophiles to self identify with the stories as being an idealization of their desires. Just some evidence of this being the online pedophile ring known as Wonderland Club and a memoir written by a NAMBLA member and sex offender from prison called *The Death of Peter Pan.*

Nabokov wrote a semi-autobiographical short story about a girl he loved as a child who died in her youth. This means little even as circumstantial evidence even alongside his authorship of the book *Lolita*. Brandon S. Centerwall in his essay "Hiding in Plain Sight: Nabokov and Pedophilia" published by the University of Texas press claims "there are adequate grounds for concluding he was.' Centerwall does concede however that "the late Mr. Nabokov's conduct toward children was, and remains, unimpeachable."

"My understanding is that he was in love with Alice, but he was so repressed that he never would have transgressed any boundaries," Alice Liddell's great-granddaughter Vanessa Tait explained in the BBC documentary *The Secret Life of Lewis Carroll*. She does however explain that the particularly explicit photograph was likely what led to Carroll being banished from the Liddell household and forced to break contact with the girls in 1863. As to what happened, perhaps the truth once lay in the missing pages of Charles Dodgson's diaries from that period.

Will Self describes Carroll as "a heavily repressed pedophile, without a doubt."

Smithsonian magazine wrote of Carroll's "shifting reputation" over the years. From the 1930s on, writers began to suggest that perhaps Charles Dodgson was, in fact, a highly repressed pedophile.

Once again, it should be pointed out that the three major biographers of Dodgson/Carroll believe he harbored pedophilic urges but did not act on them. As for what it was that led to the break with the Liddell family, biographers can never know for sure seeing as four of the thirteen volumes of his diaries from around the time the Liddells no longer welcomed him into their home have mysteriously disappeared. It is believed that a descendant of Dodgson actually cut them out after the author and mathematician's death.

A note written by one of Dodgson's nieces suggests the break occurred due to rumors that he was courting either the young girls' governess... or one of the eldest of the girls. Laurence Irving, a son of one of Dodgson's friends recapped gossip referring to him as a "greying satyr in sheep's clothing." Then again, Will Brooker indicts our times and culture saying, rumors about his possible urges "say more about our society and its hang-ups than it does about Dodgson himself." Jenny Woolf, author of *The Mystery of Lewis Carroll* puts it well:

"We see him through the prism of contemporary culture—one that sexualizes youth, especially female youth, even as it is repulsed by pedophilia."

The Victorian era was certainly an era of great sexual repression, but the Cleveland Street Scandal didn't occur in a vacuum. As an example let's head to jolly olde England of the Victorian era.

A supposedly sexually repressed era where a sort of "cultural pedophilia" was in vogue, as mentioned in the academic essay "'Oh, doll divine': Mary Pickford, masquerade, and the pedophilic gaze." Victorians "simultaneously eroticized and angelized prepubescence bubbled beneath the propriety and restrain on the surface of the time."

As a result, the idea of pedophile rings extending to the highest rungs of society shouldn't be so surprising. A homosexual brothel featuring children supposedly engaged as "telegraph messenger boys" actually being patronized by the highest echelon of British society is scandalous indeed. Equally scandalous is the fact that this story was completely unknown to the general public until March of 1975. Prince Albert, who some have theorized may have been aided by the court surgeon in enacting the Jack the Ripper murders, was very closely intimated in the conspiracy of the mass theft of innocence in Decadent fin de siecle England.

The *New York Times* a few years ago ran a full-page spread commemorating Irish playwright, poet, Decadent and Dandy Oscar Wilde. Wilde was, in their opinion, an icon and martyr for gay rights. Best known now for his *The Picture of Dorian Gray*, Wilde is as well known for his flamboyant lifestyle and razor-sharp, sardonic wit as he is for his famous banishment from England. Wilde's exile was necessitated by a scandal that involved Wilde "buggering" a young member of the Upper Class, Lord Alfred Douglas, son of the Marquess of Queensbury. Douglas Murray's *Bosie: A biography of Lord Alfred Douglas* relates that at one point the Marquess, enraged, expressed that his son ought to have "the shit kicked out of him."

Like the prototypical Dandy himself, Beau Brummell, Wilde was not "born of the manor" per se, however, he rose quickly to success. As a young man he found himself in the most popular and elite social circles as his star rose over London's West End playhouses. As quickly as his star rose, it plummeted due to fallout from the aforementioned scandal.

Now Douglas, unlike the poor Irish poet, was Lorded gentry, which makes the turnabout all the more interesting considering the Judge's pronouncement. Wilde's first trial was a defamation case brought against Queensbury. Wilde was faced with the accusation from Queensbury of "posing as a sodomite." It was this trial that brought up the letters between Wilde and Bosie (Queensbury's son) that had Wilde convicted.

The third and final trial of Oscar Wilde saw him tried for acts of "gross indecency" of the type he was accusing the Marquess of Queensbury and enacted upon Queensbury's son. Over 120 cases of gross indecency of this type had been tried at the Old Bailey and Wilde's was extraordinarily unusual as far as severity. Was Wilde being especially punished for his role in absconding client lists from Cleveland Street? Had Wilde crossed some invisible line, not through his outrageous behavior, but through threatening to uncover the salacious and outrageous behavior of others, including those in the court?

According to records from the Old Bailey Courthouse, Wilde was being extorted. Surely, many Lords were as well. The Cleveland Street Scandal was the Franklin Cover-Up of its day and would not have been broke in the first place had not a frightened messenger boy admitted the sex work cover operations when discovered with an inordinate amount of change in his pocket. 4 schillings at the time would have been several weeks earnings and the police were investigating "a theft" at the time, so thanks to self-preservation the brothel was finally closed. Wilde was not being extorted by a rent-boy however. Wilde was in fact "protecting himself" vis a vis certain "stolen items." Is it possible certain "stolen items" could have (as they finally did in the 70s) implicate persons such as the "Honorable Hamilton Cuffe," who would prosecute Wilde in 1895 as Director of Public Prosecutions.

In *The Picture of Dorian Gray*, Wilde would seem to allude to the actions of the Ripper murderer and the Cleveland Street Scandal. Both Arthur Conan Doyle and Oscar Wilde were even approached to write about the Ripper killings. The killings ended after the suicide of John Pruitt, an Oxford colleague of Wilde's. Wilde didn't believe the current official story that Pruitt was the murderer, pointing out that he was a lawyer, not a doctor as the Metropolitan Police Criminal Investigation Department had claimed. Wilde also pointed out that Pruitt's suicide was more likely precipitated by the discovery of a relationship he had with a schoolboy that had just been found out.

Multiple people, including author Gyles Brandreth advanced Ripper theories. Brandreth's based on letters from George R. Sims, Victorian-era journalist following the Ripper case and first cousin of Brandreth's grandmother. Brandreth, and some others believe Wilde may have known more about the Whitechapel Murders than he let on. For anyone familiar with *Programmed to Kill: the politics of serial murder*, Dave McGowan's work on the potential connection between serial killers and elite pedophilia rings, this should send shivers down your spine.

Anyway, as far as Cleveland Street goes, perhaps these half-veiled intimations were what led to the notoriously awful reception. One reviewer slyly admitted the book was suitable for "none but outlawed noblemen and perverted telegraph boys." Despite the cover-up, the Cleveland Street Scandal had, thanks to "journalistic innovations of the day" forever cemented in its contemporary readers the vision of certain Lords having their perverted way with poor boys. In fact, Wilde's sodomy trial would *have* to focus on "the rent boys" considering Victorian England would not allow such impropriety as a Lord and a low-borne to become the talk of the town.

According to a Guardian book review of *The Trials of Oscar Wilde*, the reviewer admits that "the prosecution only made progress when it introduced the rent boys' evidence." The same rent boys who, it would be found out 8 decades later were involved in the sex scandal that should have rocked several of the Lords as well as a handful of Royals?

"Bunburying" is a term from *The Importance of Being Earnest* referring to using an assumed name while leading a double life. The practice echoes somewhat the dual lifestyle of Dorian Gray, Dr. Jeckyll, and Mr. Hyde and, perhaps the Ripper murderer or murderers themselves.

LGBT publication *QX* magazine writes of the Cleveland Street Scandal:

"A watch was placed on 19, Cleveland Street, and, sure enough, 'a number of men of superior bearing and apparently of good position' were recorded knocking in vain at the door. Chief Inspector Frederick Abberline, who had failed the previous year to catch Jack the Ripper, reported that the visitors included at least two MPs and Lord Arthur Somerset, Assistant Equerry to the Prince of Wales. There was enough evidence to make further arrests. But nothing happened. Why? This is where the story gets really juicy.'"

Somerset's solicitor, Arthur Newton, "quietly let it be known," says McKenna, "that any prosecution of Lord Arthur would mean that the name of a very important person would be dragged into the scandal." The Assistant Director of Public Prosecutions named this VIP as none other than Prince Albert Victor, eldest son of the Prince of Wales, grandson of Queen Victoria. Was Newton bluffing to keep his client out of court? "If Eddie [the Prince's family name] was involved nobody will ever know," Chandler admits. "If he went to Cleveland Street, he went there in disguise." Significantly, however, Somerset never said in so many words that Eddie wasn't one of Hammond's clients.

Arthur Newton was also a client of the Cleveland Street brothel as well as defending Wilde in court against sodomy charges. Newton would show up in court again:

One more trial was to arise as a result of the Cleveland Street scandal in respect of the activities of Arthur Newton. The next was related to defense solicitor to the aforementioned Arthur Somerset who, it was believed, had helped Somerset evade justice. Newton was brought before the court on the 12th December, 1889 and charged with conspiracy to pervert the course of justice for allegedly interfering with witnesses and arranging their disappearance to France.

He was convicted but received the relatively mild punishment of six weeks in prison. He was even allowed to resume his legal practice, representing the author and playwright Oscar Wilde in his trial for gross indecency with other men five years later in 1895.

As you see, even in the courtroom, Wilde was literally surrounded by boy-buggering bluebloods and despite this, his trial resulted in far harsher punishment than any to date for the same charge. According to the book, *Oscar Wilde's Scandalous Summer: The 1894 Worthing Holiday and the Aftermath*, Charles Gill, Charles Willie Matthews, H.H. Asquith and, Frank Lockwood show there were also ties between the Cleveland Street Scandal and the Oscar Wilde trial.

If those "stolen items" were indeed documents related to the Cleveland Street Scandal and/or Jack the Ripper murders, this could have been, along with clues left in his final works the real reason for the severity of his punishment. His last two plays were still playing in the West End when he saw his final court date. *The Importance of Being Earnest* about two men leading double lives and *Lady Windermere's Fan* features the main character "sacrificing their reputation." If Wilde *is* a martyr, could it be as one of the first researcher casualties of the Pedophacracy?

Cleveland Street was far from the end of institutional pedophilia in the UK though. Despite it running rather rampant at least the instances are occasionally investigated to a greater degree than similar cases in the US.

Wilde by the way was influenced heavily by Joris Karls Huysmans. In the introduction to the Decadence from Dedalus edition of J.K. Huysmans' *La Bas,* Robert Irwin puts Huysman's exploration of fin de siecle occultic investigation in context. Irwin mentions the occultists Charles Naundorff and Vintras, rumors of connections between Bourbon royalty and Freemasonry. Another important aspect of *La Bas* is the Abbe Boullan and defrocked priest, cult leader and alleged child murderer Joseph-Antoine Boullan. Boullan was part of Huysman's entry into the darker side of the occult world after having more than flirted with the Rosicrucian secret society. The backdrop of Theosophy, secret societies, child murder, and secret Satanists within the Catholic Church obsessed Huysman to the extent that after his exploration and the Roman à clef and thinly veiled biographical drama he spent the last of his days cloistered on church grounds fearing for what he'd seen and heard rumors of. Stories of Satanist priests and child sacrifices would haunt him to his dying days.

THE CIA's MK-Ultra EXPERIMENTS AND TRAUMA TRAINING

The CIA's inhumane experiments on unwitting soldiers, civilians, and children are often claimed to have been inspired by Nazi scientists imported via Project Paperclip. The truth is these types of experiments predate WWII. G.H. Estabrooks attempted to create "super spies" with alter personalities. One of his most famous victims was Candy Jones who was subjected to trauma training and hypnosis.

Paul Verdier, psychiatrist, and hypnotist was the author of *Brainwashing and the Cults: An Expose on Capturing the Human Mind*. "It must be accepted that brainwashing... is now being used here [in the United States] by devious persons with personal gain in mind." Neither Verdier nor Estabrooks, however, ever used the term "mind control" which would be more associated with the MK-Ultra program which would build on the research of Wendell Johnson's Iowa University "Monster Experiment" involving psychological torture applied to children, the psychological torture of Candy Jones, and other experiments that presage the Nazi mind control experiments.

According to Verdier: "an individual's voluntary conscious self-control [will] be bypassed or short circuited." This occurred by circumventing the brain's "cortical block." Euphoric drugs, isolation, solitary confinement, and "the most dramatic and unique item in the brainwashing arsenal" hypnosis were described by Verdier but also employed in the CIA's MK-Ultra experiments.

According to Verdier, pain, and fear were some of the best tools for trauma training. According to Russian political scientists, Verdier said, "given enough punishment, all the people in any time or place are susceptible to hypnotic control."

Verdier mentions the research of Neurologist Dr. Wilder Penfield, who discovered that "sensations of pain from the muscular sensory system enter the sub-cortical brain regions directly." Penfield, by the way, was also involved in MK-Ultra along with Dr. Ewen Cameron of McGill University where the Bronfman sisters who bankrolled Keith Raniere's NXIVM sex cult were educated. Even the cult's personal physician, Dr. Brandon Porter, was a McGill alumnus. There were several universities and research centers that repeatedly worked with the CIA covertly on inhumane and illegal experiments. Sometimes involving children.

The Bronfmans made it to the top through murder and rum-running from Canada to the US during the prohibition era. John McCain divorced his dying wife to marry into the Hensley fortune. The Hensley's, of course, were going into the alcohol business. Bronfman, if you didn't know, is Yiddish for Whiskey man. Naturally, after the end of prohibition, the Bronfmans went into legitimate liquor and beer distribution. Speaking of coincidences, Jack Ruby may have been connected to the Jewish side of the mob. Ruby, by the way, was also visited by MK-Ultra scientist Dr. Louis Jolyon West who comes up a few times in this story. Just another coincidence, I'm sure.

Many of the same names and institutions come up time and time again. The Bronfman family of the Seagrams fortune is one such name. Bronfman money helped support the cultish "psychic mafia" that surrounded CIA sponsored scientist, Dr. Andrija Puharich in the 1970s in the same way that Bronfman whiskey and organized crime money propelled McCain's career, funded paranormal research, and kept afloat "the Vanguard," Keith Raniere.

Apart from the Clintons, Keith Raniere's NXIVM cult had attracted the Seagrams heiresses Sara and Clare Bronfman. The Bronfman clan were famed bootleggers with connections to Meyer Lansky of the Jewish mob before the family went legit. The Bronfman crime family was also instrumental in supporting John McCain's role in Arizona politics.

Nancy Salzman and the Bronfman sisters were also members of the Clinton Global Initiative in addition to being NXIVM VIPs. Although the story only made headlines in recent years, the abuses are not at all a new occurrence. 15 years ago Kristin Marie Snyder committed suicide. She was last seen leaving a NXIVM course and the note she left behind indicts the cult:

"I was brainwashed and my emotional center of the brain was killed/turned off."

The cult also had some other pretty shady dealings. For one Raniere, AKA Vanguard, was known to have groomed and bedded at least a few underage girls. In addition to that were the psychological experimentation on unsuspecting victims perpetrated by a doctor involved hearkens back to the heyday of the CIA's MK-Ultra mind control research. The cult used a "brain cap" that attached electrodes to the scalp during some of these experiments which involved viewing simulated rape, real beheadings and other horrific scenes.

How did NXIVM manage to stay underneath the radar for so long? The answer is, they didn't really. As far back as 2007, the *New York Post* reported on the cult and how they were run out of Arkansas during Bill Clinton's tenure as governor. The same article also pointed out how the cult and its members had sunk thousands of dollars into Hillary's presidential campaign over a decade ago. Most of the NXIVM donors were first-time political donors and were giving them the $2,300 maximum donation amount.

As far back as 2012, a *Times Union* article labeled the group an "extreme cult" after news of the cruel and unwarranted psychological experimentation first broke. Recently, the state Department of Health dismissed two separate complaints related to the cult's experiments (which involved branding and psychological abuse) under the auspices of Dr. Brandon Porter who has since been arrested for illegal human experimentation. The Office of Professional Medical Conduct however argued that the "issues you describe did not occur within the doctor-patient relationship." In other words, since the cult doctor was acting as a "cult doctor" at the moment rather than as a personal practitioner supposedly nothing unethical occurred.

Dr. Ewen Cameron and McGill were just one of many researchers and institutes involved in mind control experiments on witting and unwitting human subjects. Ironically, former President Bill Clinton even made a public apology about the US's role in Canadian mind control research.

So, because the cult already had some powerful connections (including politicians like the Clintons, Richard Branson, Oprah, Jay-Z, and even a member of the Dalai Lama's entourage) maybe the better question is how is it they were finally stopped? Well, it most likely has to do with one of the victims being the grandaughter of Catherine Oxenberg. She not only starred in the TV show *Dynasty*, but she's also a scion of one somewhat. The eldest daughter of Princess Elizabeth of Yugoslavia formerly married to a close personal friend of the Kennedy family. Evidently, it takes someone connected to a Dynasty to take down a group connected to so many other dynasties.

Dr. Laurette Bender was also involved in LSD experimentation. Primarily on children. She was inspired after an early professional conference regarding the drug in 1960 sponsored by the CIA front group, the Josiah Macy Jr. Foundation. Dr. Harold Abramson, the allergist who was attending physician to Frank Olson before his surreptitious dosing with LSD and subsequent assassination, was a presenter at the conference.

One experimental drug popular with CIA contractor Dr. Robert Hyde, was Metrazol. Supposedly for use in controlling aggressive behavior, but some patients, including Karen Wetmore, received the drug with no explanation given. Metrazol use at the Vermont State Hospital was correlated with a ten-year rise in fatalities "patient deaths skyrocketed." Finally, in 1982, the FDA took Metrazol off the market.

In 1955 and 1956, Dr. Bender had first heard of the use of psychedelics in children with autism, schizophrenia, and other disorders. Bender had previously worked with electroshock therapy which was also commonly used by contractors connected to MK-Ultra, Project Artichoke, and other mind control projects and subprojects.

Families of unfortunate test subjects of Dr. Ewen Cameron's CIA sponsored MK-Ultra mind control research are considering a class-action lawsuit. The CIA's MK-Ultra program ran from 1953 to 1976 officially. Among the declassified files are the descriptions of psychological horror and grossly unethical human experimentation, often on unwitting test subjects. The family of the deceased Phyllis Goldberg says she's spent the last 20 years of her life as a "complete vegetable" regressed to the stage of a literal infant and unable to care for herself at all. A far cry from the bright and ambitious 19-year-old nurse to be ruined by the MK-Ultra program.

She was to be treated for "mild depression" but ended up a part of Dr. Cameron's cruel experiments. After this, Phyllis could barely stand to be touched.

"When you went to pat her, just as a gesture, she would cringe," Levenson said. "That bewildered me – not realizing, or understanding, she had electric shock equipment put on her head so many times that it [remained] in her subconscious."

Dr. Cameron was surprisingly honored as the first chairman of the World Psychiatric Association, and also served as president of both American and Canadian Psychiatric Associations. The CIA recruited him to help with research after being intrigued by his "psychic driving" theories which they felt could be used to "break" spies. Cameron was paid around $69,000 between 1957 and 1964 to conduct MK-Ultra related research into mind control. The experiments combined LSD, shock therapy, paralytic drugs, medically induced comas and there are also allegations of sexual abuse.

Since the statute of limitations is up, families are seeking punitive damages and a public apology. 77 former MK-Ultra patients were compensated in 1992, but some were not eligible as they could not definitively prove that their lasting psychological damage (which ran the gamut from incontinence, amnesia, and childlike regression) came from the unauthorized and largely illegal experiments of Dr. Cameron.

In the previously mentioned Dr. Verdier's final chapter, "Benevolent Brainwashing in the Future" he explains his belief that mind control "used effectively and economically to solve many of society's pressing human problems, until now, has seemed virtually unsolvable." So the unspeakable torture of children, adults, mental patients, civilians, and soldiers was apparently collateral damage "for the greater good" according to the researchers who worked with the CIA.

Some of the experiences of MK-Ultra victims and the methods of their medical torture bear some resemblance to the testimonies of certain alleged victims of "ritual abuse."

FALSE MEMORY SYNDROME FOUNDATION

The False Memory Syndrome Foundation is a motley crew of unlikely partners. A mixture of well-respected academics, adding the cachet of respectability. Some of whom incidentally were also CIA-funded MK-Ultra researchers The roster includes Dr. Louis Jolyon West who happens to show up alongside MK-Ultra victim, "the Unabomber" Ted Kaczynski, Timothy McVeigh and Jack Ruby's side. Especially when "delusions" (like that of McVeigh's claim of being controlled by a microchip implant) need to be dispelled. West also showed up during the Patty Hearst trial.

The False Memory Syndrome Foundation was a group seemingly formed to discredit claimed victims of incest and ritual abuse. In addition to the handful of CIA-funded psychiatrists on its roster including Dr. Louis Jolyon West there were more than a few suspected pedophiles. One example are the Eberles, authors of *The Politics of Child Abuse.*

Paul and Shirley Eberle, like other members of the False Memory Syndrome Foundation, attempted to prove the explosion of child abuse cases that were being reported were almost certainly faked. The Eberles, by the way, had been charged with child pornography distribution before writing their book on how child abuse, in general, was overblown and ritual abuse was non-existent. Their pornographic publication *Finger* featured illustrations of sex with children, articles about rape and pedophilia and published letters from proud pedophile readers. The LAPD investigated them for possible child pornography distribution but this was rarely brought up when they were engaging with the media on the topic of the supposed moral panic manifesting in incest and other child abuse cases popping up throughout the 1980s.

Despite their dubious past, they were cited as authorities on the "myth" of an epidemic of child abuse in the United States. Alleged child pornographers, mind control researchers, pedophile apologists and multiple individuals accused of child abuse and incest banded together and became a powerful lobby to discredit the idea of ritual abuse. Despite this, the United Kingdom's Department of Health in 1994 claimed ritual abuse was by no means a "myth."

The spokeswoman of the group was Dr. Pamela Freyd. She and her husband were stepbrother and sister before they married at age 18. Like many of the members of the FMSF, she had a personal stake in proving that children were manufacturing false stories of abuse based on implanted memories by overzealous psychiatrists and therapists. Then there were a few who were almost certainly pedophiles themselves such as Ralph Underwager who was scandalized after the following quote from June of 1991 from Dutch pro-pedophilia journal *Paidika* went public:

"Paedophiles can boldly and courageously affirm what they choose ... I am also a theologian and as a theologian, I believe it is God's will that there be closeness and intimacy, unity of flesh, between people... paedophiles can make the assertion that the pursuit of intimacy and love is what they choose. With boldness, they can say, 'I believe this is in fact part of God's will.'"

Underwager was asked to step down from FMSF because he would not disavow the statements believing it was not borne out by science that sex with children was harmful to them.

Despite the shadow over many of the FMSF alumni, they were taken very seriously for years. One example where they both spoke to the press and were involved in a case of child abuse took place in Canada. The classic tactic of victim blaming was apparent:

"Little girls have to learn that their fathers are off limits when it comes to gratification of sexual feelings," Dr. Richard Gardner claimed to the *Toronto Star* speaking on behalf of the False Memory Syndrome Foundation in the article "Incest: Stop the Nonsense and Get to the Difficult Truth."

Another FMSF luminary was Elizabeth Loftus, whose false memory research has been regarded by memory researchers as influential, but increasingly controversial. Many of her original claims are of late being regarded as over-stated. Rather bizarrely, another member was stage magician, entertainer, and celebrity skeptic, James Randi.

Underwager was one of the founders of both FMSF and VOCAL (Victims of Child Abuse Laws). He claimed "60% of women" sexually abused in childhood reported the experience was "good for them." An interesting figure since he thought that 2/3 of child abuse allegations were falsified. If the FMSF and VOCAL founder is to be believed, only a minuscule portion of victims of child abuse are actually harmed by molestation. VOCAL even lobbied to "overhaul child abuse reporting" that would curtail mandatory reporting requirements in Florida.

Despite this, Underwager was an "expert witness" in over 200 cases of sexual abuse of children from the United States and Canada to Great Britain, New Zealand, and Australia. Psychologist Anna Salter has published scholarly work on errors in his research. Underwager attempted several lawsuits all of which failed.

Despite their general skill at manipulating media and often the court system, not everyone was so convinced by the group.

Reporter Steven Elbow changed his tune on the FMSF over the years after hearing from a victim. He wrote about this in his article "Rethinking the False Memory Controversy":

"The case was not only being watched by the group, it was being publicized. A Wisconsin member of the foundation gave me a call to tip me off to the case, then put me in contact with executive director Pamela Freyd, who offered compelling quotes and easy research for a reporter trying to cobble together a quick and interesting story. It never occurred to me that I was dealing with a highly organized public relations machine until a victim and a sexual assault advocate emailed me with their concerns.

I can't blame them for being a little disappointed."

Elbow spoke to "Beth", (not her real name) a victim of child sexual abuse, for Madison, Wisconsin's *The Capital Times*:

"It just came to me," she told Elbow in *The Cap Times*

"But the memories were fragmented and didn't make a lot of sense. So she talked to her brother about it.

He said, 'Yes, I did it,' and he also sexually abused my sisters. Most incest survivors don't have a perpetrator that will ever admit that they did something.'" .

Beth, went on to earn a Ph.D. in women's studies with a focus on incest survivors. This is similar to Dr. Jennifer Freyd, the daughter of the step-siblings accused of allowing incest to scar their daughter's psyche.

"I'm sure my parents have gone (to the False Memory Syndrome Foundation people) to say, 'Oh, woe is us. Our daughter is crazy and she's always been crazy.'" Beth said.

Elbow points out that "although the false memory people don't like to admit it," there are "numerous cases of repressed memory" borne out by eyewitnesses, DNA evidence, or even confessions. Beth told Elbow that the guilty parties will often use anything to protect themselves, including playing the victim themselves. With the help of a well-heeled and well-organized PR machine like FMSF backing them countless court cases were likely skewed by FMSF's supposed expert witnesses.

"It really is a lot of perpetrators and a way for them to squelch the issue," Beth said.

One case where the FMSF gave aid in an incest abuse case was covered in the *Toronto Star*. Harold Merskey testified on behalf of a doctor accused by a woman of sexual abuse. This although the doctor had confessed to abusing her and others. Was he suffering from "false memory syndrome" too?

Jennifer Freyd, who accused her father of sexual abuse during her teen years, not only held firm to her word but became a well-respected memory researcher herself at the University of Oregon. In her book *Betrayal Trauma*, she points out how children, as part of their survival, have to believe their parents will keep them safe. This is one of the mechanisms that leads them to bury incidents of abuse as a coping mechanism. This sort of dissociation based on trauma was a key part of MK-Ultra programming and predates MK-Ultra.

Dr. G.H. Estabrooks wanted to create "alter" personalities to create a spy who couldn't reveal information even under torture. To do so he employed "trauma training" protocols.

In the PBS *Frontline* documentary *Divided Memories,* Pamela Freyd refers to herself as the "public voice" of FMSF. She points out how anyone accused has the "right to defend himself or herself" and have their accusations "examined." She claimed to aid people who were falsely accused. Their goal was simply to let these falsely accused people, victims of therapists, and doctors dredging up false memories, to share their side of the story. To be fair, there are almost certainly cases where with the aid of hypnosis, memories have been implanted. This was, after all, one aim of the MK-Ultra mind control experiments.

As for the power of the "false memory lobby," Mike Stanton, Pulitzer-Prize winning journalist, said in a 1997 article in the *Columbia Journalism Review*:

"Rarely has such a strange and little-understood organization had such a profound effect on media coverage of such a controversial matter," Stanton wrote. "The foundation is an aggressive, well-financed PR machine adept at manipulating the press, harassing its critics, and mobilizing a diverse army of psychiatrists, outspoken academics, expert defense witnesses, litigious lawyers, Freud bashers, critics of psychotherapy, and devastated parents."

The Foundation was, if anything, effective. Former FMSF spokeswoman Freyd says the number of cases of false memories has fallen precipitously as litigation has changed psychiatric practices.

"If you look at meetings, for example, of professionals, it used to be back in the 90s that a third or a quarter of the sessions would be involved in recovering memories of sexual abuse," says Freyd. "You don't see that anymore."

Besides, Freyd went on, the internet had already spread far and wide the (often erroneous) information about repressed memories that was formerly shared to thousands of parents each year accused by their children of abuse.

"The world has changed," Freyd said.

When asked if that meant "mission accomplished," she curtly replied.

"I think we can slowly disappear."

Before they did that they certainly left a mark. As previously mentioned, vocal members of the group were Pamela and Peter Freyd, the married step-siblings accused to this day of abuse by their daughter, Dr. Jennifer Freyd. The book *Blind to Betrayal,* by Dr. Freyd details how Pamela Freyd wrote a thinly veiled, "anonymous" account of her daughters alleged false accusations, changing enough detail to cast aspersions on her daughter's character, but not enough to make the account truly anonymous. She then posted the article, with a letter from herself on FMSF letterhead to Professor Freyd's professional colleagues, identifying Freyd and attempting to undermine her, just at the time she was being assessed for promotion.

Professor Freyd then recounts that, some of her colleagues, rather than being turned off by such a gross misuse of power, instead joined the Advisory Board. In a further twist, Pamela Freyd then eventually invited her own daughter onto the FMSF Scientific and Professional Advisory Board.

The original Philadelphia group would eventually go international. By 1993 the Australian False Memory Association was formed. One of their leading spokespersons was Dr. Gerome Gelb who gained some attention after a plagiarism scandal and then was arrested for taking a loaded handgun into a Melbourne magistrate's court in 2007. He had been suspended from practice twice, once for having sex with a patient, and later for the firearms charge.

Eventually, the idea of "false memory syndrome" was mostly discredited. At the end of December 2019, headlines rang out "Survivors Celebrate the End of the False Memory Syndrome Foundation:" As it turns out, "false memory syndrome" may itself have been false.

Despite their successful PR, Dr. John F. Kihlstrom's false memory syndrome "has never been ratified as an actual diagnosis." They were, however, fairly successful in their attempts at discrediting victims of childhood sexual abuse and incest for years. FMSF finally disbanded at the end of 2019. It was far past due in the minds of many academics such as Dr. Michael Salter who believed "no such syndrome" existed to begin with.

Upon learning from Dr. Michael Salter, a researcher in the area of sexual abuse and complex trauma, about the dissolution of the FMSF, survivors celebrated the end of the organization. Many pointed out how the organization's influence negatively impacted their lives as sexual abuse survivors.

THE FINDERS

The idea of sadistic abuse of children is something no ordinary human wants to contemplate. The case of Peter Scully, the Australian who viciously, violently and sadistically sexually assaulted numerous children is not an isolated incident. As the *Irish Times* reported, reprinting a front-page story from Italy's *Corriere della Sera*:

"From our comfortable seat in life... we never could have imagined that thousands of well-off adults, integrated and even cultured, find pleasure in seeing children tortured and killed."

One problem with pinning down what is ritual abuse is the definition itself. That and those who are handling the cases. Kenneth Lanning of the FBI Behavioral Science Unit from 1981-1996 was the FBI representative to the Missing and Exploited Children Task Force from 1996-2000. He had this to say in his "Satanic, Occult and Ritualistic Crime: A Law Enforcement Perspective:"

"This definition may have value for academics, sociologists, and therapists, but it creates potential problems for law enforcement.

"Certain acts engaged in with children (kissing, touching, appearing naked, etc.) may be criminal if performed for sexual gratification. If the ritualistic acts were performed for spiritual indoctrination, potential prosecution can be jeopardized, particularly if the acts can be defended as constitutionally protected religious expression. The mutilation of a baby's genitals for sadistic sexual pleasure is a crime. The circumcision of a baby's genitals for religious reasons is most likely *not* a crime. The intent of the acts is important for criminal prosecution. The author has been unable to precisely define ritualistic abuse and prefers not to use the term. It is confusing, misleading, and counterproductive. Certain observations, however, are important for investigative understanding."

So there you have it, the federal view on ritual sexual abuse from the man in charge of missing and exploited kids. And what happens to some of those kids? Well, it's impossible to say for sure, but we can look further into a case mentioned throughout the book. That of the Finders.

Despite mainstream media reports that the idea of organized child exploitation is no more than fake news, the truth is, documented evidence exists to show that the situation is not only not fake it's not even particularly new.

In the mid-1980's a major case of child abduction, abuse, and exploitation was on the verge of being blown sky high when out of the blue, none other than the Central Intelligence Agency ordered the children involved returned to the shady men with the van. The men in the business suits were found with several naked children who witnesses described as "feral" when they were arrested, officials found pornographic images of the children, pictures of the children playing with recently slaughtered dead animal parts and documents pertaining to means of procuring children as well as evidence of a major plot to export trafficked and exploited children worldwide.

The Washington Post offered some initial coverage in February of 1987:

"Authorities investigating the alleged abuse of six children found with two men in a Tallahassee, Fla., park discovered materials yesterday in the Washington area that they say points to a 1960s-style commune called the Finders, described in a court document as a "cult" that allegedly conducted 'brainwashing' and used children 'in rituals.'

"D.C. police, who searched a Northeast Washington warehouse linked to the group, removed large plastic bags filled with color slides, photographs, and photographic contact sheets. Some photos visible through a bag carried from the warehouse at 1307 Fourth St. NE were wallet-sized pictures of children, similar to school photos, and some were of naked children.

"D.C. police sources said some of the items seized yesterday showed pictures of children engaged in what appeared to be 'cult rituals.' Officials of the U.S. Customs Service, called in to aid in the investigation, said that the material seized yesterday includes photos showing children involved in bloodletting ceremonies of animals and one photograph of a child in chains. Customs officials included Agent Bob Harrold who had coordinated from New Orleans with BNDD and Baltimore authorities intercepting drug shipments. Customs said they were looking into whether a child pornography operation was being conducted."

According to U.S. District Court records in Washington, a confidential police source had previously told authorities that the Finders were "a cult" that conducted "brainwashing" techniques at the warehouse and the Glover Park duplex at 3918-20 W St. NW. This source told of being recruited by the Finders with promises of "financial reward and sexual gratification" and of being invited by one member to "explore" satanism with them, according to the documents.

```
PAGE FIVE DE RUCNFB 0179 UNCLAS

COLUMBIA, WASHINGTON, D.C., WHO DECLINED PROSECUTION FOR VIOLATION
OF TITLE 18, U.S. CODE, SECTION 1201 (KIDNAPING) AND 2251 (SEXUAL
EXPLOITATION OF CHILDREN).  WMFO SA [       ] WAS THE WMFO            b6
CASE AGENT IN THIS MATTER.                                            b7C
     DOJ REVIEW OF USCS DOCUMENTS INDICATES THAT DURING THE
EXECUTION OF THE SEARCH WARRANTS BY THE MPD AT THE TWO "FINDERS"
PROPERTIES, USCS SA [       ] CLAIMS TO HAVE OBSERVED A
SUBSTANTIAL AMOUNT OF COMPUTER EQUIPMENT AND DOCUMENTS
PURPORTEDLY CONTAINING INSTRUCTIONS FOR OBTAINING CHILDREN FOR
UNSPECIFIED PURPOSES.  THE INSTRUCTIONS ALLEGEDLY INCLUDED THE
IMPREGNATION OF FEMALE MEMBERS OF THE COMMUNITY, PURCHASING
CHILDREN, TRADING CHILDREN AND KIDNAPING THEM, [       ] CLAIMS      b6
                                                                     b7C
                                                                     b7E
```

Despite some brief bits of press about the notorious cultish group often referred to as The Finders very little information exists about the group today. Once the CIA closed the case out, the children were returned to the Finders. This despite images depicting the children being involved in bloodletting rituals, signs of sexual abuse, and claims from the children that they were only given food as a "reward." The Tallahassee PD and Customs documents also refer to children being "ordered" from Hong Kong, further evidence that the Finders were involved in some sort of widescale child exploitation and trafficking racket.

Before you get the idea that a shadowy group of pedophiles infesting our government ended in the era of the so-called Satanic Panic bear in mind the somewhat recent discovery of multiple members of Hillary Clinton's State Department being found in possession of child pornography at their government office desks, no less. Even more recently, the revelations of the sick predilections of Huma Abedin's Pakistani IT aide. Huma herself, of course, is married to Anthony Weiner who was, himself convicted of "activity unbecoming" to use a Prince Andrew euphemism, involving minor children.

And it's not just the exploitation of children, horrific enough as that is, the fact that so little media exposure or follow-up occurred despite the major national security breach, this constitutes. If members of our government are involved in such monstrous activities (and time and again enough have been caught to prove this is so) then the possibility of widespread blackmail operations is what, in national security jargon, is referred to as a clear and present danger.

Marion Pettie was married to an intelligence agent, but also had a friend you may be familiar with. Maybe you know already that Patch Adams was more than a character from a feel-good movie starring Robin Williams. The real-life Patch Adams was, surprisingly enough, a close friend of Marion Pettie, the central figure behind The Finders.

When two members were discovered with 6 small children. The nude children were described as extremely dirty and "feral" and had been living in the van with the two men from the Finders. The men claimed they were taking the children from DC to Mexico to a school for gifted children. Why they detoured into Tallahassee on their way to Mexico is anyone's guess.

PEDOGATE PRIMER

Once the two Finders cult members were arrested, an investigation began that uncovered documents related to procuring children (from purchasing them outright to kidnapping and trading), evading authorities by multiple means (including moving from jurisdiction to jurisdiction). U.S. Customs was called concerning nude pictures of some of the children. When the police apprehended the two men, one produced a business card that stated that "the bearer knew his constitutional rights to remain silent and that he intended to do so."

Despite evidence of potential child trafficking, telex messages related to "the purchase of two children in Hong Kong" and another telex involving "bank secrecy" the investigation was closed out and the children returned to their abusers when the CIA decided to make the Finders case an internal investigation.

From the Tallahassee Police Department's investigation notes:

FBI FACSIMILE COVERSHEET

WASHINGTON METROPOLITAN FIELD OFFICE
SQUAD C-4 (202) 252-7844

PRECEDENCE
- ☒ Immediate
- ☐ Priority
- ☐ Routine

CLASSIFICATION
- ☐ Top Secret
- ☐ Secret
- ☐ Confidential
- ☐ Sensitive
- ☒ Unclassified

Time Transmitted: _____
Sender's Initials: _mc_
Number of Pages: _____
(Including Cover Page)

To: _FBI HQ_
(Name of Office)

Date: _11/3/93_

Facsimile Number: _(202) 324-3089_

Attn: _SSA _____ VC4, CID_
(Name Room Telephone)

From: _SAC, WMFO_
(Name of Office)

Subject: _"FINDERS" GROUP_
WSTA - SEXUAL EXPLOITATION OF CHILDREN;
OBSTRUCTION OF JUSTICE — P.I.
OO: WMFO

Special Handling Instructions: _PLS HAND CARRY TO SSA _____
ATTACHED IS A MEMO LOCATED IN THE WMFO FILE ON FINDERS DEALING
WITH THE STATEMENT/MEMO OF CUSTOMS AGENT _____ FOR YOUR
INFORMATION_

Originator's Name: _SA_____

Telephone: _X 7792_

"On Thursday, February 5, 1987, Senior Special Agent Harrold and I assisted the Washington D.C. Metropolitan Police Department (MPD) with two search warrants involving the possible sexual exploitation of children. During the execution of the search warrants, numerous documents were discovered which appeared to be concerned with international trafficking in children, high tech transfer to the United Kingdom, and international transfer of currency."

After they were arrested, evidence of child pornography and wholesale kidnapping and exploitation were recovered. Documents involving the sale of children to overseas buyers and more evidence weren't enough to hold them when the CIA closed down the investigation explaining that it was now an internal affairs matter.

But what does all this have to do with Patch Adams? Hunter "Patch" Adams is closely related to Marion Pettie and the Finders. Patch Adams was a close friend of Marion Pettie's and had been a tangential member and even seen members as the group's "personal physician." According to Adams, there was no instance of child abuse among the Finders and no pedophiles among the members who were by and large "over-educated" eccentrics.

Adams spoke with the *Rappahannock News* in defense of the Finders cult: "I'm embarrassed for the news media. They really made a mistake here. I can see a giant legal case coming out of this."

Of course, no such "giant legal case" ever came out, but the Finders were freed to continue whatever it is they were working on. At least one of the small children showed signs of sexual abuse, Adams' explanation:

"I just can't imagine the Finders tolerating sexual abuse. If it should turn out that a child has been abused, it's a private problem with a member of the organization with the organization unaware of that problem."

As for Marion Pettie himself and the Finders as a whole, Patch had this to say:

"Marion Pettie [is a] very intelligent, extremely well-read, a perceptive thinker who gathered around him over-educated people who find current society, as I do, not very interesting. They dropped out of whatever it was they were doing to play games under Pettie's direction. The anthropological, psychological, sociological game of life with each other. Never to my knowledge have they done drugs of any kind. They like playing games, more in their heads than in their hearts. This is not Scientology. I know lots of Finders who have left. We get together. We laugh and joke about it. They're probably laughing about all this right now. Marion Pettie is not an angel. He's not a devil. He's a regular person unless a regular person is someone who is bored with his job, his life and is dissatisfied with his life. If that's the definition, then I guess he's not a regular person."

Considering this close connection to a group many feel was involved in weaponizing child exploitation for the national security state. Perhaps it was this that fueled those wild rumors about Camp Gesundheit near Mt. Droop and Hollywood producer Jon Robberson's claim that Robin Williams was blackmailed into making the movie *Patch Adams*.

Franklin Scandal

Academic turned journalist, Nick Bryant, recently revived some interest in the Franklin Scandal. Despite the story disappearing, like so many others before and after it, Bryant's story offers evidence that there was indeed a Cleveland Street Style "messenger boy scandal" among DC VIPs and other elites that went as far as the victims being given "private tours" of the White House after hours.

His book is disputed as a "reliable source" according to the Wikipedia Talk page for the Franklin Scandal entry. This even though *Vanity Fair* found him credible enough to interview him. As for whether or not the Franklin Scandal allegations are unfounded, Bryant explained:

"Well, no one has ever sued me. 'The Franklin Scandal' is layered with corroboration and vetted by an attorney. I told Trine Day, my publisher, 'You guys have got to really vet this. What we are saying about a lot of people is pretty horrific. I am confident I am telling the truth here, but you've got to vet it.' So, it was vetted by an attorney and no one has ever accused me of libel over the years it has been out. No one has ever accused me of fabricating anything. It's a very solid piece of investigative journalism.

"Publishers were just not interested in the story at all. When I would bring this story to publishers and editors, I could sense their cognitive dissonance. 'He's talking about horrific crimes, so either I have to do something about this or label him as crazy or a conspiracy theorist'. So, that's the reputation that I gleaned in New York after pitching "The Franklin Scandal" to everyone. They would rather write me off as a conspiracy theorist or crazy than take Franklin seriously. I took it to just about every major editor in New York. After I pitched Franklin to them, they weren't returning my emails. So, that was a tough way to go.

"Given my inherent skepticism of conspiracies, I initially dismissed the tales. Eventually, I came across a number of stories about a cult called the 'Finders' that weren't rooted in fringe paranoia, but, according to the sources, in a US Customs report."

In Dec 1993, *U.S. News & World Report* (which at the height of the CIA media infiltration program code name Mockingbird, refused to play into the propaganda game) began investigating the scandal again. In Congress, Democratic Representative Charlie Rose of North Carolina and Florida Representative Tom Lewis, a Republican, would work to expose the government's ties to the Finders. "Could our own government have had something to do with this Finders organization and turned their backs on these children?" asked Representative Lewis in the article. "That's what all the evidence points to. And there is a lot of evidence. I can tell you this: We've got a lot of people scrambling, and that wouldn't be happening if there was nothing here."

Bryant interviewed Monsignor Robert Hupp who was affiliated with the Boy's Town chapter connected to the incident. He also talked to the child pornographer and Lawrence King associate, Rusty Nelson. During the investigation and writing, he received a threat and warnings. At one point, with the aforementioned Nelson, he was pulled over and his vehicle searched by police.

The "fastest rising, black star of the Republican party" Larry King, was never found guilty of anything but financial crimes related to the Franklin Credit Union. Paul Bonacci, an alleged victim won a civil suit though he never received a penny of the million dollars of damages payment he was awarded.

"Republican VIPs started distancing themselves from King like rats fleeing a sinking ship" after the Franklin Credit Union raid. Before it, King was close to then-Vice President George Bush by his word. Bush would contest this himself.

A controversial Supreme Court Justice, himself accused of sexual harassment by more than one woman, would come to defend King though. Clarence Thomas stood by King calling his legal issues "unfortunate." Thomas, by the way, was also on the invitation list of one of King's DC parties in 1987, despite claiming to have not met him until 1988 at the New Orleans Convention. That said, King was apparently a fundraiser like no other. The connections don't end here though. Clarence Thomas' wife grew up in Omaha and was an aide to Congressman Hal Daub, who was on the Franklin's Advisory Board, also benefiting from King's fundraisers and campaign contributions.

Angela Wright was the second Thomas subordinate who had been subpoenaed. She would have been able to corroborate Anita Hill's testimony of inappropriate behavior and sexual harassment... if she had been called after being flown from North Carolina to DC to testify as she was initially asked to. Senate Judiciary Committee Chairman Joe Biden claimed that the subpoena was lifted at the wishes of Wright and her attorney. This claim is "adamantly" denied by those parties. As a result, the supposed "he said, she said" affair went nowhere and Thomas squeaked through on a 52-48 Senate vote.

Another important figure in the Franklin affair is Charlie Rogers whose life was shortened by a suspicious suicide at 29 years old. Bryant "found substantial corroboration connecting Rogers and King." Rogers was found dead on November 10, 1986. His front door was locked with no sign of forced entry at that point, but the third-floor deck was left unlocked. Rogers' family disagreed with the official claim that it was suicide.

Rogers was a bodybuilder and bouncer at The Max, a popular gay bar that King was found in often. At the scene of his death, a gold deerskin coat was found along with a receipt showing that Larry King had purchased it for $2,810. King had also sent "dozens of flowers" and a "closet full of clothes" and an 18-karat bracelet with Charlie emblazoned on the top and "From the Boss" engraved on the inside.

3 weeks before his death, Charlie offered a free ticket to DC to his mother because he had decided not to use it. His mother later claimed she felt he was trying to broach the subject that would lead to his death and regrets not being receptive. Rogers would take the

flight. Leaving Omaha 11:25 AM, layover in Minneapolis, arrive at DC at 4:35 PM, and then leave DC the same day at 8 PM, to return to Omaha just before 11 PM.

Rogers had confided in his little sister that he thought he was in trouble and also hinted at a double life but said he couldn't go into details for his family's safety. He did however mention that it was due to his connection to a powerful man by the name of Larry King. He said he had received around $50,000 from King who was connected to even more powerful individuals. He said he wanted to make a clean break with King. He left his sister's house after that, leaving a stationery card with Larry King's name on the front. She would never see him alive again.

When it was reported that he was dead, Rogers' sister told their mother he had told her he was afraid for his life and that if anything happened to him to contact Deputy Attorney Bob Sigler. Sigler claims he had no idea why he was to be contacted and that their only connection was handling a few misdemeanor cases while he was in private practice.

A reporter for the Warren Buffett-owned *Omaha World-Herald*, James Allen Flanery, looked into the situation, talking to Rogers' family. Flanery had also researched another suspicious suicide related to a former Boy's Town student who may have been connected to King's affairs. Flanery requested Rogers' autopsy report but the Sheriff's Office, which was generally open about such requests, denied him the report.

Warren Buffett, by the way, was implicated in a debt, "a burden at times" according to former Congressman John W. DeCamp, who initially helped break the story, both on the Congressional Record and in his book *The Franklin Cover-Up*. Buffett, DeCamp told former-CIA director William Colby, along with Ronald Reagan, Vice President George H.W. Bush, and Democratic presidential candidate Bob Kerrey (at the time Salomon Brothers head and the second richest man in America) all were connected to Larry King. DeCamp, like Bryant, would receive warnings and death threats.

Peter Citron, a reporter with *Omaha World Report* was also implicated. McGowan wrote that "the investigation led to the doorsteps of some of the most powerful men in Omaha, including newspaper publisher Harold Andersen (a lunch partner of George Bush), local columnist Peter Citron, a judge, the mayor of Omaha, the city's Games and Parks Commissioner, a prominent attorney, the former police chief of Omaha, businessman Alan Baer, and multi-billionaire Warren Buffet (for whose son King sponsored a political fund-raiser)."

Flanery's eventual report on the King-Rogers connection wouldn't appear in the *World-Herald* until over two years after the death. It also neglected to mention the black book found after Rogers' death or that King had contacted the family requesting a beeper that Rogers had for work. Flanery called one of the numbers in the black book, left his name and number, and the sister of the man he called responded saying he had stumbled upon a national prostitution ring.

Bryant also reached out to the alleged victims and their family to talk about what the grandmother of two of the girls referred to as "horrible things" they had to take part in. Repeated beatings Tracy and Tasha experienced for years were corroborated by her sisters and "a trove of documents from Nebraska's Department of Social Services (DSS)."

Beaten by an extension cord or other items for everything from getting a C or lower in school, folding their clothes improperly, using the phone without permission, chewing gum, even "making noise when shutting off a light switch" could earn a beating. At times of course, there were beatings that occurred with no specific cause. One DSS document reports how all the foster children were forced to line up and watch one, naked, as he was whipped.

The physical abuse accompanied emotional and psychological abuse. Jarrett and Barbara "had an unorthodox arrangement with the DSS." They received state subsidies for all eight adopted and foster children in the home, in part because the children all came from (already) troubled homes.

Barbara Webb, cousin of Larry King, foster mother of the children religiously attended Omaha's Seventh Day Adventist church every Saturday. She sang in the choir and brought the children who would sometimes get dressed up to go to church or attend events with "Uncle Larry." The kids would also sometimes run into Uncle Larry at the North Omaha Girls Club meetings of which King was president.

One of the foster children, Eulice, said that these gatherings "gave her the creeps" and that the functions included approximately fifteen "older men" who "seemed to salivate over the twenty or so teenage girls who were present."

Barbara Webb at one point received a large handbag full of VHS tapes. When they were out on the town one night, they had forgotten to lock their bedroom door. The children found the videotapes and played them. All featured teenagers engaged in explicit sex acts.

Bryant has also looked into both the Finders Cult child abuse case, as mentioned above, that ended in a CIA internal investigation and the Jeffrey Epstein story. Referring to the "road map to that network in Epstein's now-infamous black book, filled with many bold-faced names, phone numbers, and addresses, from Donald Trump, Bill Clinton, and Ehud Barak to Alec Baldwin, Ralph Fiennes, Mick Jagger, and even Courtney Love" this star-studded collection of influential persons forms "a mosaic of Epstein's social contacts," Bryant told *Vanity Fair*.

Bryant's connection to the Epstein case began nearly a decade ago and by 2012 he had acquired a copy of Epstein's black book, which had gone public after feds caught an Epstein employee trying to sell it for $50,000.

Bryant referred to that black book as "a template for what's happening now and how high up it goes. A major parallel between the two stories is that Lawrence King, who was one of the primary pimps of this pedophile network I wrote about, and Jeffrey Epstein, they were both flying children interstate, and they had both done it with impunity for a number of years.

In both instances, you have officials who were unwilling to back down. In Epstein, you had the Palm Beach Police Department that was unwilling to back down, and in Lawrence King's case, you had the Nebraska Senate unwilling to back down. Epstein had an island, and I'm sure he had these parties also at his place in Manhattan and elsewhere, and there were hidden cameras. In this particular venue in Washington, DC, where the Nebraska victims were trafficked, there were also hidden cameras.

The individual who owned the house in Washington, DC, he had intelligence affiliations. We're seeing with Epstein that he also had alleged intelligence connections. King and Epstein collected children in the same type of fashion. King would have kids conscript other kids, just like Epstein would have kids conscript other kids. In both cases, the victims were threatened and hassled. Both Jeffrey Epstein and Lawrence King had lavish lifestyles, but there wasn't an obvious explanation for their wealth, and both were prominently associated with power brokers of the highest order." *Vanity Fair* made sure to append that statement with the following 'editor's note.' "A grand jury concluded there was no evidence to charge King."

Bryant considers the Epstein case to be small potatoes compared to what occurred with the Franklin Scandal. That "the pandering network was much, much bigger" than that of Epstein. He also puts King down as only one half of the "pimp" staff in the interstate child sex ring. King was procuring children from foster homes and Boy's Town Orphanage. Meanwhile, Craig Spence in DC had his house wired with audio and video recording equipment to compromise visitors who partook in their parties.

Bryant explained to *Vanity Fair* how social services would eventually find out, but even after going to both state and federal law enforcement, they found their stories ignored. King would be found guilty in court of embezzling $40 million from the Franklin Savings and Loan he was manager of. This sort of situation would repeat itself somewhat when Dennis Hastert would be sentenced for illegally structuring payments to underage boys he molested, rather than for the crime of child molestation.

King would also be ordered to pay $1 million in damages to Paul Bonacci. As mentioned before, Bonacci never saw a dime of this. Soon after, a sub-committee was formed to look into King for his financial corruption, Social Services personnel backed down from their stories themselves. Stories of torturous abuse, cocaine, and other drug use and powerful people most often including Larry King who was possibly "at the center" of transport in planes in his name and paid for out of his pocket. A pocket fat with ill-gotten gains and overflowing into the campaigns of political brass.

Bonacci, incidentally, may have been involved in the case of the first of the missing children on a milk carton, Johnny Gosch. The 2014 documentary *Who Took Johnny* implicates an Omaha child trafficking ring.

Omaha and Houston (to this day a major hub of human trafficking) may have been part of a network used by John Wayne Gacy. WGN Chicago, in 2016, put forth the possibility that in addition to serial murder, Gacy was part of a human trafficking ring that specialized in young boys. Gacy, coincidentally also had friends in high places, both in politics and law enforcement.

Bonacci claimed after being victimized by the ring he ended up drug-addicted and recruited into kidnapping "throwaway kids and virgins." Bonacci had details about Gosch and his mother that were not entered into the public record or mentioned in the news. Bonacci was also said to have experienced multiple personality disorder, similar to the dissociative states brought about by G.H. Estabrooks style "trauma training." John DeCamp, in addition to leading the charge against King, was the lawyer for Bonacci.

Bryant and DeCamp both explain how even after being accused of perjury, Alisha Owens and Paul Bonacci (who were facing 160 and 60 years respectively in prison for perjury) wouldn't back down from their claims. The investigation led to Rusty Nelson at this point, who Bryant believes was a key part of the blackmail operation as a photographer. Rusty claims to have given pictures from some of the child sex parties to Caradori that could bring down not only King but much more powerful people who would gather in Chicago or DC. Bryant touts "four points of corroboration, other than Nelson" of this claim's veracity. When Caradori made his flight back to Lincoln, Nebraska, his plane *broke apart*.

In Chicago, he met with Rusty Nelson, who was a child pornographer and, according to Bryant "also, I think, a blackmail photographer. I spent a lot of time with Rusty. He's kind of an unsavory guy. But in an investigation like this, you have to spend a lot of time with unsavory people. It's just the way it is."

Bryant says after a bit of digging, he noticed some "very strange things" regarding the Caradori investigation that led all the way up to the FBI and even the National Transportation Safety Board. Bryant has few doubts that Caradori's death was a homicide.

The Senate sub-committee hired Gary Caradori who found additional victims, recorded their testimony, and brought it once again to state and federal law enforcement. Shortly after that Gary Caradori would die. His plane "disintegrated" over Lee County, Illinois. The plane's wreckage was "strewn over a ¿ to 1 mile stretch" and the NTSB investigator finally admitted, "the fact that the wreckage is scattered over a large area certainly demonstrates that it did break up in flight."

According to Caradori's brother, he had told him he had just come into possession of, once again, a little black book full of addresses and phone numbers which "if they knew he had it, they'd kill him." Caradori's family also says that the wreckage is missing several key items, most importantly Caradori's briefcase with much of his notes. The rest of his records would be impounded in under a day's time by the FBI.

Senator Loran Schmit suspected the plane was sabotaged and ordered a private investigation into the cause. William Colby, director of the Phoenix Program and the man who gave Douglas Valentine his entrée to the cloak and dagger world, was selected by his friend DeCamp to lead the inquiry. Colby had been a former CIA director whose intelligence career went all the way back to the Office of Strategic Services (OSS) in WWII.

Colby, "an avid outdoorsman" would be found dead in an apparent single person canoe incident... with sand weighing down the back of the canoe so it was easily found. A documentary produced by his son Carl Colby, *The Man Nobody Knew*, examines the mysterious circumstances of his father's death. It is controversial, even among Colby's family, for suggesting perhaps he committed suicide. Regardless of what the actual circumstances (hypothermia related heart failure being the official cause) there are certainly several people who have questioned whether or not Colby's death was natural or if foul play was involved.

In between the initial flash (and fade) of interest due to the *Washington Times* article, then DeCamp's Congressional investigation and book, the Rose and Lewis investigation, and *U.S. News and World Report* article in 1993, and Bryant's book is the ironic silencing of the documentary *Conspiracy of Silence*.

On Tuesday, May 3rd, 1994, a documentary made in Yorkshire, England about the Franklin Scandal was scheduled to appear on the Discovery Channel. *Conspiracy of Silence* even showed up in the *TV Guide* and news listings, but by the time it was ready to appear something had transpired as it never aired. Discovery Channel never offered a reason why the quietly suppressed documentary never aired, but considering the established and long-standing connections between the highest levels of government, the security state and the media, it is not so much a stretch to say that it was squelched to prevent the story from getting out.

The documentary deals with Larry King and Boy's Town and their involvement in the scandal it refers to as a "continuing cover-up at the highest levels." DeCamp himself featured in the documentary calls the incredible story "a web of intrigue" that "spreads out like a spiderweb through Washington DC" right to the White House and "involves some of the most respected, powerful and richest businessmen in this United States of America."

DeCamp himself had spent time at Boy's Town as a child. It is a tragic fact that such a respected institution, immortalized in a 1938 film featuring Spencer Tracey as Father Edward J. Flanagan and Mickey Rooney as an indigent who is saved from delinquency by Boy's Town, would fall into such disrepute.

The children were allegedly involved in drug dealing, used as mules, and (reminiscent of Cleveland Street again) couriers in addition to their use as sex slaves. Father Flanagan and Boy's Town, was a home for orphans since WWI. At the time of the documentary it had

500 children, was funded to the tune of 500 million dollars annually, not counting the 30 million worth of donations coming in each year which made it "the richest square mile in the world" according to the documentary. Boy's Town in Omaha was its own incorporated town and served as its own school district, its own diocese.

Boy's Town had a private account at Franklin Credit Union. It was overseen only by a privileged few bookkeepers. Father Val Peters, then-head of Boy's Town, looked into the allegations of a sex ring after the embezzlement was discovered. The children wouldn't talk though and the evidence wasn't turned over to authorities. The sex parties continued.

Larry King shows up in several reports from foster homes that showed up at DSS, "at least a foot high" worth of material where his name's appearance was continually ignored. DeCamp points out that "with control of three or four elements," top levels of the media, the justice department, and the police "you can make right wrong, you can make truth, falsehood, falsehood truth" with them in your hands "you own the system." The same system that locked away evidence forever sealing it by court order after they found they were being looked into by outside parties. DeCamp compares the case to Watergate and Iran-Contra. Pointing out that in all cases, it is the media, not the corrupt systems involved in covering up wrongdoings of themselves and their subsidiaries. And with a cooperating media, any sort of cover up is possible.

ABUSE OF THE CLOTH

For decades, priests and even bishops and other officials in the Catholic church and even Vatican were implicated in the abuse and subsequent cover-up of children, often multiple children. For most of the decades of that abuse, there was a virtual blackout in the news. To this day, the church pays out millions to buy silence and spends millions more on legal fees to avoid paying alleged victims of child sexual abuse.

Despite this, the situation shows no signs of abating. The number of reported cases quadrupled in 2019 compared to the five previous years. To look at the bright side, we should consider the possibility this doesn't mean more cases of abuse, merely more *reported* cases of abuse. In 2019 alone, over 4,400 cases were reported in the US. Just over 1/3 of those cases surging ahead are due to multiple dioceses creating compensation funds for victims whose cases had passed the statute of limitations to sue in their state, according to the US Conference of Catholic Bishops.

It was difficult to initially break the story due to the influence and money of the Church. Now that the genie is out of the bottle, the cover-up and shuffling around of offenders is as damning as the crime. In late August of 2020, it was reported that when a low-ranking parish priest was asked to give evidence against an archbishop accused of covering up child sexual abuse he was "mysteriously summoned to the Vatican" where he was "quizzed" by the Pope regarding what he would say.

As of December 2019, the amount that the Catholic Church may need to pay out surpassed $4 billion. Though the largest number of alleged cases and the bulk of media attention in the past 20 years has been centered around the Catholic Church, several other denominations have had multiple scandals as well.

The *Houston Chronicle* and *San Antonio Express-News* revealed the story of over 700 known victims of 380 trusted Southern Baptist preachers, youth ministers, and deacons. Dozens of churches were aware of the abuse by a pastor, employee, or volunteer but continued to employ them. There was also a disturbing silence on the mission front. Once again, the investigation showed that internal records of the allegations were kept from the public. Over 100 Southern Baptist youth pastors are also either in prison currently or registered as sex offenders after charges of sexual crimes.

This is likely just the tip of the iceberg. In the case of sexual assault especially when power is abused, often the victims are afraid to come forward for several reasons. Not least of which is the fear they won't be believed or that nothing will come of their charges. This seems to have been the case here.

The Southern Baptist Convention doesn't nearly have the money of the Catholic Church, one of the richest organizations in the world. They were still able to hush up and shuttle around abusers for years with near impunity, however.

In addition to the respect of the clergy and the fact that children are often trained to unquestioningly comply with their preachers, priests, and other clergy. The matter of confidentiality is also an issue that makes it easier for predators to continue to operate, protected behind the veil of secrecy conferred by the cloth.

One recent example of this involves a woman in Oregon suing the Church of Latter-Day Saints. The plaintiff's lawyer responded to *Time* magazine via email regarding a reported case of a father sexually abusing his daughter:

"This has nothing to do with victims of abuse. This case is different because the confidentiality of a church member making confidential statements to a clergyman which are privileged."

Oregon, by the way, is one of around 28 states in which clergy are required to report suspected incidents of child abuse or neglect.

ABC News in 2019 also reported on highly-situated members of the LDS infrastructure being alleged to have been involved in the abuse of children. A bishop of the church claims that when the father of an abused boy went to him he didn't specifically mention the sexual abuse but that he was already counseling the accused Mormon.

"I have my son's word against Michael Jensen's word," the child's mother told ABC news. "And not even my bishop, my Relief Society president, none of these people are supporting me. The only thing that I could think of for my son was I don't want to go to the police because I have to put him through this questioning."

The boy's mother initially declined to report the case to the authorities because she didn't want to put her son through the difficult process of cross-examination on the stand. Until, that was, she heard about another investigation of Michael Jensen's abuse of more children.

In the past few years, MormonLeaks and a documentary from HBO have opened the doors on some of these cases. There were even allegations of an LDS Victims Hotline being used to squelch any sexual abuse claims before they could cause the church embarrassment.

LDS members may fear coming forward due to a lack of support from the church. If a bishop vouches for an alleged predator or "discerns" that they are telling the truth, LDS members are asked to unquestioningly follow the advice of their bishop even if it means not reporting a crime to authorities. In some cases, bishops will absolve abusers who have "repented." The church's version of released on recognizance. Taking a page from the Vatican, the Mormon church will also occasionally transfer abusers to different churches. In some rare cases, the abusers may be excommunicated but even then the abuse is likely to go unreported to authorities outside the church.

As much news as the Warren Jeffs case made, it might be easy to blame only fringe fundamentalist offshoots of the LDS for this type of behavior. Sadly that is not the case at all.

LDS bishops like Timothy McCleve, Michael Wayne Coleman, Erik Hughes, Todd Michael Edwards, and Lon Kennard, Sr. were offered prison sentences for sexually molesting multiple children under their authority.

"It seems to show that the Church's main concern is its image and the aftereffects of this abuse, as opposed to the focus being on the victims," Ryan McKnight, founder of MormonLeaks said. The MormonLeaks documents gave an unprecedented, behind the curtain view of the process when missionaries and even a stake president were accused of sexual abuse.

The Seventh Day Adventist church, certain Hassidic communities, and other major Christian denominations have also been embroiled in such dark scandals. Religion provides a nearly perfect cover for the activities of predators. As one survivor of childhood sexual abuse in the SDA church points out "Sexual abuse in church communities is as rife as in the secular world. That's because churches are made up of human beings - all are flawed by sin. Predators often see the cloistered order of the church community as a happy hunting ground."

As with the LDS community, there are several cases of abuse both within the traditional church as well as in the more fringe offshoots. The Branch-Davidian sect in Waco was purportedly sieged to protect the children from sexual abuse. This claim is belied by the fact that the federal government's actions resulted in the deaths of many of those children. As with many other cults with charismatic leaders, such as Keith Raniere's NXIVM, sexual abuse of minors was involved. Scientology founder L. Ron Hubbard spent his last years aboard a ship in international waters surrounded by "mainly pubescent girls."

Jehovah's Witnesses have also been marred by multiple child sexual abuse scandals. In just the past few years, much has been done to raise awareness about many of these churches' members and clergy abuses of children and the resulting coverup. Jehovah's Witnesses were sued over "historic sex abuse" early in 2020.

Jehovah's Witnesses have a policy of not punishing, or often even reporting, child sexual abuse unless either a second witness comes forward corroborating the child's claims or the abuser confesses. A former elder had admitted to the recurrent issue of authorities not being called in. The man had gone on to become a church elder himself but eventually decided to report his abuser to the police only to discover he had gone on to abuse other children and died in prison a year earlier.

According to a solicitor representing some of the former members in the UK, they only sought compensation after realizing that asking for an apology was all for naught. The Jehovah's Witnesses church was intent on "denying what has happened or refusing to engage." Sarah Champion, chair of a cross-party group of MPs looking into claims of historical institutional abuses said she had "very serious concerns" regarding the open-door system allowing child molesters "back into a community where they have access to vulnerable people." She met with elders of the church. They "believe that there is more than enough safeguarding in place" despite admitting they "couldn't think of an example when they would go to the police about their concerns." As a group, they felt child sexual abuse was "a sin that they need to deal with internally." Apparently, they weren't dealing with that quite well.

The Atlantic reported on a "secret database" of child molesters that the community had kept quiet for decades. As a result, the Jehovah's Witnesses may have been in possession of "the world's largest database of undocumented child molesters: at least two decades' worth of names and addresses -- likely numbering in the tens of thousands -- and detailed acts of alleged abuse, most of which have never been shared with law enforcement, all scanned and searchable in a Microsoft SharePoint file."

A former member of the church, who for years only went by a pseudonym "John Redwood" slowly leaked some of the worst of the contents of a box of stolen documents. In one case a church member was disfellowshipped (a form of ex-communication) three times. The offender was most recently allowed back in the fold in 2008. This despite claims he had "allowed his 11-year-old stepdaughter to touch his penis" multiple times. Yes, you read that right, the onus was put on the small child, not the adult abuser.

According to the girl herself, she was only 8 when her stepfather first molested her. "I thought I didn't have any choice," she said. It was two years before she was finally able to speak to her mother about it. Her mother reported it to the congregation's elders who called in the girl... and her molester, to pray over them. Oddly enough the man was not disfellowshipped for these activities but for "fornication," "drunkenness" and "lying." For the alleged molestation, he was only "privately reproved."

The A&E investigative docuseries *Cults and Extreme Belief* featured an episode on the claims of six decades of Jehovah's Witnesses putting known child molesters in positions of authority. In addition to this, Jehovah's Witnesses prison ministry attracts several child molesters to the church according to Watchtower whistleblower Barbara Anderson who was a 43-year member of the Jehovah's Witnesses. Her position as a writer of the Watchtower tract gave her access to interior church documents that other members were not privy to.

After an article about dealing with child sexual abuse, letters began pouring in from members. At this point, Anderson began to realize the extent of the issue. In the past six years, more and more stories have been coming out.

News reports from various sources began to flow in about a seemingly neverending stream of church members, sometimes elders or other authorities in the church implicated in child abuse. Take this into account along with the organization wanting to escape scandal and you have a perfect recipe for continuing complicity in numerous cases of child sexual abuse around the world.

The Jehovah's Witness church infrastructure is "a closed shop" according to one man who says he was abused sexually from the age of nine until he was According to him, the church was "inadvertently" protecting the abusers.

Another church community that is perhaps even more closed off than the Watchtower Society is Brooklyn's Haredim, ultra-Orthodox Hasidic Jews. As the *New York Times* reported in 2009:

"For decades, prosecutors in Brooklyn routinely pursued child molesters from every major ethnic and religious segment of the borough's diverse population. Except one.

"Of some 700 child sexual abuse cases brought in an average year, few involved members of the ultra-Orthodox Jewish community — about 180,000 followers of Hasidic and other sects who make up the largest such cluster outside Israel. Some years, there were one or two arrests or none."

Suddenly the numbers began to spike. But why? For the first time in ages, the Haredim were finally allowed to go to authorities about sexual abuse rather than just reporting such crimes to their rabbis. For decades, informing authorities about a crime could result in ostracism from the community. The Haredim are similar to the Amish or Mennonites in that they take strict adherence to their religious laws very seriously and, as a result, their lives are stripped of the trappings of modernity.

It wasn't so much that the Haredi community was more prone to child sexual abuse than other groups, but the veil of secrecy served to protect predators in the same way as the Catholic Church and Jehovah's Witnesses protected predators for so many years.

An editorial from *Jewish Week* in 2008 criticized the possible politicization and protection from the district attorney's office, whose approach had ranged "from passive to weak-willed."

Many rabbis were supportive of the change while another rabbi "mentioned frequently on blogs" cited an antiquated religious doctrine that allowed the murder of someone who informs on another Jew to gentile authorities.

Rabbi Yehuda Kolko was a teacher at a Jewish school and little came of the claims of former students that he had sexually abused them. The allegations "were dismissed by rabbinical authorities" until *New York* magazine covered the story in 2006. Following the magazine write up, the district attorney's office finally filed sexual abuse charges against Rabbi Kolko but the decision to recommend probation in exchange for a guilty plea to child endangerment didn't sit well with everyone in the community.

Assemblyman Dov Hikind, who represents a predominantly Orthodox section of Brooklyn, asked victims to call into his radio show about the "epidemic" of unreported abuse of children. For half a year, he received hundreds of calls.

Change continues to come, however slow, though there is still some blowback and resistance. In 2012, an *NYT* headline proclaimed "Ultra-Orthodox Shun Their Own for Reporting Child Sexual Abuse."

After a family learned their mentally disabled son was being abused in a Jewish ritual bathhouse in Brooklyn they went to the police. Shortly afterward, their landlord kicked them out and their answering machine began to fill with angry messages and threats for their audacity at turning in another Jew to authorities. Despite "glimmers of change" some who come forward still face "intense intimidation from their neighbors and from rabbinical authorities."

According to *Canadian Jewish News* in 2016, statistics show between one in three to one in five girls and one in five to six boys in the Hassidic community are victims of abuse. Most commonly the abuser is a close family member.

Jewish Community Watch (JCW), a watchdog group, argued that Halachah (Jewish law) "very clearly" indicates that Jews are "permitted, even 'obligated' to go to secular authorities" when someone presents a danger to the community.

Like the Hasidic Jews, the Amish live a life intentionally isolated from modernity. Also, like the Hasidic Jews, there is a great distrust of the larger culture outside or "the English" as the Amish refer to outsiders. *NPR* spoke with Sarah McClure in January of 2020 about her year-long investigation into Amish child sexual abuse.

McClure mentions 52 cases that were prosecuted but that this is nowhere near an accurate number from her experience. As has been seen in multiple instances before, those brought to authorities are likely only a small percentage of the total cases:

"The majority of my sources never made a police report. They never had a court case. Whenever I spoke with these women, they had dozens of other victims that they told me about, dozens of other cousins and friends and family members that - they told me that this had happened to them, too. And, obviously, I can't put a number out there that's unverified or not supported or corroborated by a court case or a police report. It's very difficult to do a story like this where the evidence is limited. And so just anecdotally, just based on my conversations with these women and men, there are a lot more victims out there in Amish country that we may never know of simply because there is no paper trail."

In a number of cases, victims who come forward about their abuse are sent away to "special Amish or Mennonite mental health facilities." Also like with the Hassidic communities, those who dare speak out are shamed, shunned or threatened.

CHILD ABUSE AND CULTS

Cults offer the same, or even greater protection for predators once again due to the stricture of obedience to authority and veil of secrecy and silence. Ruth Wangerin, is the author of *The Children of God: A Make-Believe Revolution?* A Professor of Anthropology at Queens College and CUNY, she "was asked so often if the Children of God was CIA-linked that I felt morally and intellectually obligated to find the answer." She pointed out that due to the shroud of secrecy behind COG she could reach no definitive conclusion. "That doesn't mean the question is answered in the negative, however-- because the more I learned the more 'coincidences' I discovered."

She points to the "cozy relationship" with several people the intel community was close with at the time including Ferdinand Marcos, the Christian Democratic Party in Italy, and the wife of the Shah of Iran. Apparently, it was also reported to her that in Peru in 1975 "it was obvious the Children of God had obtained military permission to be able to hand out leaflets." They showed up in Libya and South America during times when the CIA was undertaking covert action.

University of Alberta professor Stephen Kent has another excuse for COG attempting to curry favor with Muammar Gadhafi:

"Especially in the early days, Berg was virulently anti-American, and that anti-American virulence fit very well with Gadhafi." Kent also claims at least one child was sired by Gadhafi and one of Berg's cult members.

Wangerin suspects "possible COINTELPRO-type sponsorship" of multiple cults including the Divine Light Mission. As implausible as CIA-sponsored cults may seem, the CIA link to Reverend Sun Myung

Moon's church, the Moonies as they were commonly referred to, is documented in, among other places, US Congressional record. South Korea, to this day, is a hotbed for cult and fringe religious activity such as the Korean Shincheonji church which was implicated in being "super spreaders" of the coronavirus. The Shincheonji church, by the way, had a presence in Wuhan before the outbreak.

Korean CIA (KCIA), which was set in place by the American CIA helped to establish Rev. Moon's cult. Moon's Washington ties don't end here, of course. Rev. Moon also founded the *Washington Times* newspaper.

COG, like Baha'i, had been accused of being connected to the CIA by several countries. COG had deep pockets (which certainly is helpful if you're aiming to cover up child abuse for decades unchecked) but "its finances were a well-guarded secret."

COG was not only accused of infiltrating various countries for the CIA, but many religious groups and angry parents also denounced how youth were exploited in such affairs as "flirty fishing." Large numbers of COG members showed up in Italy in 1975 and 1976 around the same time the CIA was donating large amounts of money to the Italian Christian Democrats and other parties whose agendas were supported by the State Department and intelligence community. The claim that David "Moses" Berg was a CIA asset was made in a large Italian newspaper in 1976. This apparently "distressed" COG members who were afraid it might affect their work in the area.

An ex-member of COG reported that The Family, as COG were calling themselves at the time, were trading sex with high ranking members of the military for "informal protection." Probably the most well-known members of the Children of God cult are River and Joaquin Phoenix and Rose McGowan. In a 1991 interview with Joe Dulce in *Details* magazine, River Phoenix was asked if there was anything he did at an early age he wishes he had waited for. His response: "Yes, make love." Dulce asked how old River was. Four, he responded.

River of course would be found dead of an overdose outside of a nightclub in LA in 1993 on Halloween night. That is only one early death connected to COG/The Family. Multiple members have alleged sexual abuse and later committed suicide or overdosed.

Ricky Dupuy, a former member, appeared on Larry King Live and admitted he had been ordered to rape a 10-year-old. He too would later commit suicide. Berg's wife was Karen Zerby. Karen's son Ricky Rodriguez also says he was sexually abused before killing himself.

Berg's cult wasn't even quiet about their penchant for child sex. Many of the Family pamphlets were related to child brides and how sex with children was actually a way to get closer to God. The perverse "Law of Love doctrine" never caught up to Berg or other leaders of the cult despite all this and the many accusations, including multiple of Berg's own granddaughters accusing him of molesting them as children. *The Guardian* reports that multiple FBI and Interpol investigations into Berg and other members' child abuse allegations ended in 1994 with his death.

Berg's adopted son Ricky Rodriguez had sexually suggestive photos featured in a handbook called "The Story of Davidito." Rodriguez would go on to kill one of the women who appeared in the handbook with him before taking his own life The daughter of Rodriguez's nanny, Sarah Kelley, opened up to *Rolling Stone* in 2005 about her molestation at the age of thirteen.

Family pamphlets make references to "Our 'Kiddy viddy show,' as Dad likes to call them." The same document goes on to mention what a "great blessing when the cameraman, floor director & dance director have all prayed together for things to work smoothly & in order before attempting such a kiddy show."

On the same page, it talks about how the cameraman and sound-audio man should "counsel together quietly among themselves about the technical part of the job so as not to distract the children or distract the teacher." Later on the same page, "After the big girls all had a turn to dance for our king & the Eden series, Techi (2) & Davida (5) loved it too! Dad says they are both real naturals at dancing!"

Perhaps the Family/COG did not have direct connections to the international intelligence community, but if not then it is a powerful coincidence that despite all this no one was ever brought to justice.

Court cases and raids against the Children of God were rarely successful. Buenos Aires, Lyon, and Eguilles, the United Kingdom, Australia, and the United States all attempted and failed to charge members often due to purported "lack of evidence."

In Eguilles, even the pamphlets were not believed to corroborate the sexual abuse alleged by so many. The Gendarmerie's investigation ended with the following comments:

"Some works [of Father David] contain texts of recommendation, drawings which appear shocking coming from the man who is now called Father David by the adults and Grandpa by the children. One can legitimately ask oneself what from amongst these books is used for the teaching and instruction of the children today, and what is no longer in use. These questions however do not constitute proof. The same applies to the attitudes or declarations of some of the children that seemed ambiguous and should be the subject of the further complementary investigation; but, as is, neither do they constitute proof."

Once again, after a lengthy investigation following the initial raids, the Prosecutor decided there was "no proof." In many cases, the investigations never even led to preliminary hearings, much less a trial. All that bloodshed and child abuse and no convictions.

Two young former members spoke to *Daily Telegraph* in 2002 saying they "were trained to say that it just didn't happen." Another former member revealed, "I do remember long classes on how to lie to systemites."

Center for Studies on New Religions (CESNUR) mentions a several year investigation that began in 1991:

"On March 31st, 1999, Supreme Court Justice John Dunford found that 'in entering the relevant premises, searching for and removing the various plaintiffs, the defendant's servants [officers of police and Community Services] and agents were not acting under any authority conferred by the warrants... but wrongfully and contrary to the law.' 62 of the children who had been removed from their families by New South Wales authorities in May 1992, initiated a civil action against DOCS (Department of Community Services). DOCS requested a mediation just as the main part of the hearing was to commence. The terms of the settlement were confidential, however, the Australian media reported 'huge compensation payoffs.'"

A similar raid in 1992 in Melbourne ended with the children being released into the custody of their parents during the investigation. After nearly two years of hearings and a taxpayer cost of between $1.5 and $10M AUD the case was ordered permanently closed.

6 weeks after Waco, The Family finally broke "years of virtual silence" by inviting reporters and religious scholars to visit the commune in La Habra Heights.

Washington Post, like Dr. Wangerin, points out how the Children of God colonies spread out even in places like "overwhelmingly Muslim Libya, apparently with approval of its leader" Gadhafi.

David Hiebert, a former member who ran a support group for ex-members called No Longer Children, told the *Post* that flirty fishing was used to curry political favor in several countries. "They would target special people -- in the media, lawyers, in the government," he says.

Like Scientology auditing, the resulting recordings could definitely compromise powerful people. The power of a cult, in a way, is its power to abuse religious freedom in certain systems. For this reason, it is fairly reasonable to assume the security state has used infiltration, or even creation, of cults as a means to achieve their aims. According to *Tampa Bay Times* and allegations laid out in multiple lawsuits "Scientology policy enabled years of child sexual abuse."

Speaking of cults called "The Family" in Australia, there is also of course the strange case of Anne Hamilton-Byrne who, by a twist of fate, is connected to Wikileaks' Julian Assange. The Family also called itself "The Great White Brotherhood," a nod most likely to Helena Blavatsky and Alice Bailey's Theosophy. Theosophy by the way has child abuse in their background as well. Blavatsky acolyte C.W. Leadbetter was accused of sexually molesting the young J.D. Krishnamurti. Though he was never officially charged, the allegations would haunt him through his life.

As for the Australian Family/Great White Brotherhood, the children in the cult were procured by multiple means, similar to the case of the Finders, some were children of cult members, some were kidnapped by quasi-legal means. The cult had at its disposal an entire hospital and conducted LSD experiments similar to the ones that took place in the US and Canada with MK-Ultra. Assange's platinum hair matches the "Village of the Damned" blonde children of the cult who were often given massive doses of psychedelics. Assange's mother, Christine, had to escape from the group which Assange's mother's boyfriend Lief was involved in.

"The Family's leadership" according to critics, including ex-members "follows a policy of lying to outsiders, is steeped in a history of sexual deviance and has meddled in Third World politics." Meddled in third world politics when they weren't abusing children, well, doesn't that sound like someone we spoke of earlier. In fact, didn't they also call themselves "The Family?"

The New Age movement was birthed in Theosophy and Aleister Crowley's Thelema. It was influential not only on the hippie movement of the 60s and the sexual revolution but also the Me Generation of the 80s. One group that was also tangentially connected to both with a pedophilia connection is the Esalen Institute. The article "Scapegoats and Shunning" is available at Counterpunch.org by the anonymous author PARIAH. The article initially appeared on the site sexandpolitics.org. The article casts pedophiles as scapegoats and victims of "sexual fascism."

"The creation of a scapegoated class ... whom no one would defend" the article argues, is necessary for authoritarianism. This class of people "are mostly in hiding, desperately afraid of sudden exposure and witch hunts."

Eventually, after a dramatic, perhaps even melodramatic, opening the anonymous author finally explains who they are talking about:

"SEX OFFENDERS! Worse, many are PEDOPHILES!"

The article at least concedes that some of these sex offenders and pedophiles aren't entirely unfairly judged:

"Of course among these sex offenders are indeed some criminals who have caused extreme harm: violent rapists of adult women as well as children. A few of them have kidnapped, tortured, or murdered their victims."

The article points out rightly that of most reported cases of kidnapping and murder of children, parents, and other family members "in non-sexual cases" are involved.

It quotes a therapist who worked with sex offenders trying to explain that so many of these child abusers are:

"'Gentle grandfathers who made one mistake in judgment years ago and fondled their grandchild. Or lonely, geeky gay men– teenagers some of them–who sought mutual sexual release with adolescent boys. Or young female teachers who succumbed to the wiles of handsome adolescent boys or girls. Or young men who got drunk and pushed their girlfriends over a line that is now called date rape.' Yet the media, police, prosecutors, and politicians continue to insist that children are in dire need of protection from serial rapists and murderers."

"The key ingredients of this scapegoating campaign," the Pariah goes on to say "are of course sex and children." The article points out that the term pedophile doesn't even predate the 1960s "as a so-called scientific construct."

It goes on to bemoan age of consent laws being raised in most countries, mourning the loss of the supposed good old days when "common law age of consent was 10 in England" or "zero in many other societies where child-brides were common." The article also bashes "the myth that underage persons are simply not capable of consent." Another target of the author's ire is the "censorship" of researchers in "intergenerational sexuality."

The author speaks highly of Debbie Nathan, however, "who exposed and virtually stopped the so-called satanic cult child sex panic."

According to Nathan, "... I have often had a sense of being intellectually and professionally marginalized, and I have experienced instances of editors killing pieces I've written about sexual hysteria because they got cold feet, as well as refusals to assign such stories."

The main area of "censorship and shunning" of course, is the depiction of "childhood or adolescent sexuality." The article goes on to defend art that portrays "the physical beauty of children or erotic aspects of their lives" which "in the face of post-Freudian revelations of the sexual lives and interests in children" should be liberated.

Another article by PARIAH conflates bigotry against Mexicans and Muslims with increased scrutiny of sex offenders crossing borders in "An Iron Curtain Is Descending." It also decries the fact that minors cannot cross the border in the US without a guardian or parent. One can only wonder why.

But who is this masked pedophile apologist anyway? There's no way to be 100% certain but we can trace back the article to the website sexandpolitics.org which was part of an initiative run in part by David Werner, a disgraced pedophile who worked for years with many respected groups in several countries.

Werner was the author of *Donde No Hay Doctor* (Where There Are No Doctors). He worked in over 50 countries as a consultant for World Health Organization, Unicef, the Peace Corps, UNDP, and UN-ESCAP and others. He received awards and fellowships from the World Health Organization and the American Pediatric Association, in addition to being a MacArthur Genius Grant recipient and receiving other awards and commendations. This was all before his "mentorship" came to light.

Werner was voted out of the non-profit group the Hesperian Foundation after being accused of molesting several young boys, many of them disabled.

"We confronted David with the accusations and told him there was no alternative to him doing anything but resigning immediately from the Hesperian Foundation," Michael Blake of Hesperian told *Knight-Ridder Tribune* in 1994.

He was accused of molesting at least 20 boys from 10 years old to puberty. Multiple board members of Hesperian admitted they were aware of Werner's "sexual activities" for several years but "maintained silence for the sake of the foundation's work."

Since the allegations of abuse took place outside of the country and the victims were unnamed police did not pursue charges saying "unless we get specific information concerning victims in our jurisdiction the department is not going to investigate." This despite a member of the foundation giving a list of 20 boys who she says were abused by Werner in what he called "mentoring."

One board member and some of the staff confronted Werner years earlier threatening to report him to police at which point Werner admitted he had, indeed, had sex with boys during his "humanitarian activities."

One former board member knew nearly a decade before the story broke resulting in Werner resigning after being voted out. They didn't go to authorities because Werner made a "fairly solemn commitment" to disengage from the molestation.

Several of the articles cited in the Wikipedia about David Werner are no longer available online. Some are only available as web archive snapshots, some have disappeared completely.

Werner's attorney Paul Meltzer told the *Washington Post* that the allegations had "been fully investigated by the police and there has been no prosecution because there is no case." This stands in stark contrast with what the police themselves said. Werner went on to claim that his break with Hesperian was due to homophobia, not his admission of sex with small children. *The Post* also revealed that more than a year after the complaint was filed, the police had not even bothered to question Werner.

After leaving Hesperian, Werner and Jason Weston formed Healthwrights. Both Weston and Werner sponsored a site about the politics of health, the aforementioned sexandpolitics.org which is no longer available online but using the WayBackMachine at Archive.org you can see that the Counterpunch article "Sexual Fascism in Progressive America: Scapegoats and Shunning" as well as articles like "It's Time to Reform Sex Offender Laws" were hosted there giving us an idea of who PARIAH is, or at least who they worked with.

The pro-pedophilia articles are housed at a site that no longer exists, but snapshots in the archive plainly mark that they are part of the Healthwrights Workgroup for People's Health and Rights. As of September 2019, the Healthwrights website announces a new book by David Werner. Healthwrights continues to work with third world children to this day.

Werner was not the only pedophile connected to organizations like UNICEF, UNESCO, and UN over the years. *The Guardian*, Human Rights Watch, and numerous others have reported on multiple instances of sexual abuse of children by UN-related groups and other NGOs and charities like OxFam. Religious groups and aid organizations partaking in the abuse of children is one of the most nefarious abuses of authority imaginable.

We don't know of course if PARIAH is Werner or Weston, but they are certainly associated with Healthwrights at least as a contributor. Little info can be gleaned at first glance. According to CounterPunch, "PARIAH lives in Canada." In another article, PARIAH complains about the difficulties of crossing borders when you're a registered sex offender.

"One group that gets very special attention are registered sex offenders, of whom there are now just over 600,000 in the U.S. The public generally approves of all measures to limit or control this group of PARIAHs, never mind the fact that few of these were violent rapists, and that many are forced to register for decades or life, long after minimal offenses–including prostitution and public sex, or in some cases even urinating in public.

"Nowhere is censorship and shunning greater than against those who would describe or depict childhood or adolescent sexuality, or mere nudity. The 'victims' of the evil perpetrators must also be protected–and projected as the spotless mirror image of their violators–at all costs–their purity and innocence asserted (even in the face of post-Freudian revelations of the sexual lives and interests of children). Anything portraying the physical beauty of children or erotic aspects of their lives must be banned. (See Bob Chatelle's excellent summaries of the impact of the child porn crusade on freedom of expression: Kiddie Porn Panic, 1993; Limits of Free expression & the Problem of Child Porn, 1997.)"

PARIAH argues that "until the 1980s, the notion that any offender would be forced to register and be tracked–and publicly shamed–for life –went against the American notions of fairness and rehabilitation." This second article from the Healthwrights associate, decries "longer and longer sentences and increasing length of parole or probation" due to the "sex panic" in the United States. Even Megan's Law is lamented by "PARIAH."

Even "formerly progressive alternative media" have failed to speak up for the child liberators (as some pedophile activists see themselves). Unsurprisingly, considering the time the article was written, "PARIAH" also speaks ill of the NBC series To Catch a Predator.

"PARIAH" does point to others, apart from Debbie Nathan who seem to echo his sentiments. Janice Irvine's *Let's Talk About Sex* from University of California Press, 2002 is quoted, blaming the "hijacking of sex education in America by right-wing Christians" and warns the "depravity narratives" surrounding sex offenders will continue "so long as there is a 'culture of stigma' on sexual topics, and so long as the 'innocent child' model of childhood prevails." Irvine says that we "must reinvent the construct of childhood" as a result. PARIAH then goes on to compare the pedophile's struggle to that of "Reconstruction era amendments that ensured equal applications to former slaves and other people of color, and after the voting rights amendments for women in the 1920s."

PARIAH dreams of a day "perhaps fifty or a hundred years from now" in which the idea of scapegoating pedophiles "will appear ludicrous." And that society will no longer be "obsessed" with sexual acts pursued with children or "making a photograph of a 17 year old masturbating" for instance.

For all the talk of marginalization, there are certainly a great deal of dueling academics along the lines of child sexual exploitation with many feeling the entire issue of pedophilia is no more than a political football to be tossed around. Many of these scholars play up the "moral panic" side of things apparently painting the idea of the pedophile as a bogeyman of sorts: as James Hunter writes in the Journal of Homosexuality:

"The 'pedophile' is discovered to be a 'social construct that floats in the thin air of fantasy.' Since the truth-value of the construct 'pedophile' approaches zero, we are confronted with the question of why he continues to be such a central and emotionally fraught aspect of American culture. The answer to this question is found in his political usefulness. Specifically, the religious right uses him to further its agenda of sexual repression, and the political right uses him to dismantle the machinery of a free society."

PARIAH's article finishes with the following addendum:

"The writer remains anonymous because he writes and is politically active in several completely unrelated social justice movements. He fears that the shunning and marginalization he describes for those who write about this topic could compromise (unfairly) his other work."

That other work almost certainly involves some position within Healthwrights considering the article originally appeared there. The article also appears in the book *Violators: No Rights for You* by "Octaevius Altair" which at Amazon is described thusly:

Fact based account of the struggle by Project Freedom Canada to protect and preserve the integrity of the Canadian Charter of Rights and Freedoms and the Constitution it is a vital part of within Canada. From a group of Fundamentalist Christians that obtained power in Canada and proceeded to abuse that power by targeting a portion of the population within Canada for the divestment of their Charter protected Rights and Freedoms and thousands of other innocent victims for imprisonment."Altair, is also the author of *Viamund the Boy Love Vampyre* and *Mr. Altair's Simple Guide to a Complicated Universe* is available for sale at WalMart.com.

SATANIC PANIC: McMartin and Presidio

Dungeons and Dragons and heavy metal music proved a useful foil for the media to pin blame on the so-called Satanic Panic as well as, in hindsight, to make the whole thing look that much more ridiculous years on. As for the actual Church of Satan, LaVey unabashedly borrowed heavily from fascist tract *Might Makes Right*. Much has been written about the materialist, selfishness, and fascism of the Church of Satan. The entirety of the 1980s seems to have been subsumed with a sort of subconscious satanism. Not to say it had anything with worshiping the devil, simply the Nietzschean or Crowleyan ideal that a man or woman has the right to do as they will so long as their will is greater than those they intend to suppress. This self-centered philosophy is exemplified in the following quote from Aleister Crowley in "The Rights of Man" from Liber AL XVII:

"There is no god but man. Man has the right to live by his own law–to live in the way that he wills to do: to work as he will: to play as he will: to rest as he will: to die when and how he will. Man has the right to eat what he will: to drink what he will: to dwell where he will: to move as he will on the face of the earth. Man has the right to think what he will: to speak what he will: to write what he will: to draw, paint, carve, etch, mold, build as he will: to dress as he will. Man has the right to love as he will. Man has the right to kill those who thwart these rights."

The satanic panic was explored in the short CBC/Radio Canada documentary "What was the Satanic Panic?" The mini-documentary recounts the "terrifying tales" of hidden satanic messages in rock and metal music, unfounded fears related to the role playing game Dungeons and Dragons and of course allegations of ritual sexual abuse, torture and even murder attributed to "underground networks of satanists."

Stories of occult rituals were central though "much of what fueled the panic was not real," CBC says. Many high profile criminal trials were, of course, often explained away by the False Memory Syndrome Foundation. The initial report would "snowball" until it "took on a life of it's own" spurred along by "overzealous interveners." Mind the loaded language here by the way, and I thought I was biased. At least I try to be a bit less sensationalist than the Canadian news report from February of 2020.

Ignoring the fact that in many of these cases signs of physical abuse, secret tunnels, and other details are all explained away. The piece plays up "wrongful convictions" and "damaged reputations." Another subject is the potential Canadian origins of Satanic Panic in the book *Michelle Remembers* by Michelle Smith and Lauren Pazder which allegedly helped Michelle recover "repressed memories."

"There was no evidence or witnesses" to Michelle's account CBC emphasizes. Pazder coined the term ritual abuse. Pazder was an expert consultant for the prosecution in the McMartin case. CBC points out the "high demand" of satanic abuse experts ignoring the FMSF's similar experts. Ken Lanning, FBI Behavioral Science Unit began helping to "debunk" the idea by invoking hypnosis and false memories. Remember Lanning also decided that certain sexual activities between adults and children are perfectly fine so long as they are part of religious practice. Those who succumb to moral panic "abandon the pursuit of facts for a more sensational fiction" according to Lisa Bryn Rundle, host of Uncover The Satanic Panic podcast.

Finally, she asks "have we learned our lesson?" Apparently not yet, because despite cases like that of the Finders, the Franklin Scandal and billionaires like Jeffrey Epstein, the molestation of a toddler by a DuPont heir resulting in house arrest, and Peter Nygard Canadian multi-millionaire, fashion mogul and trafficker accused by his sons of having them raped occasionally surfacing, there are still weirdos, myself included, who feel that child abuse and trafficking is occurring at epidemic levels.

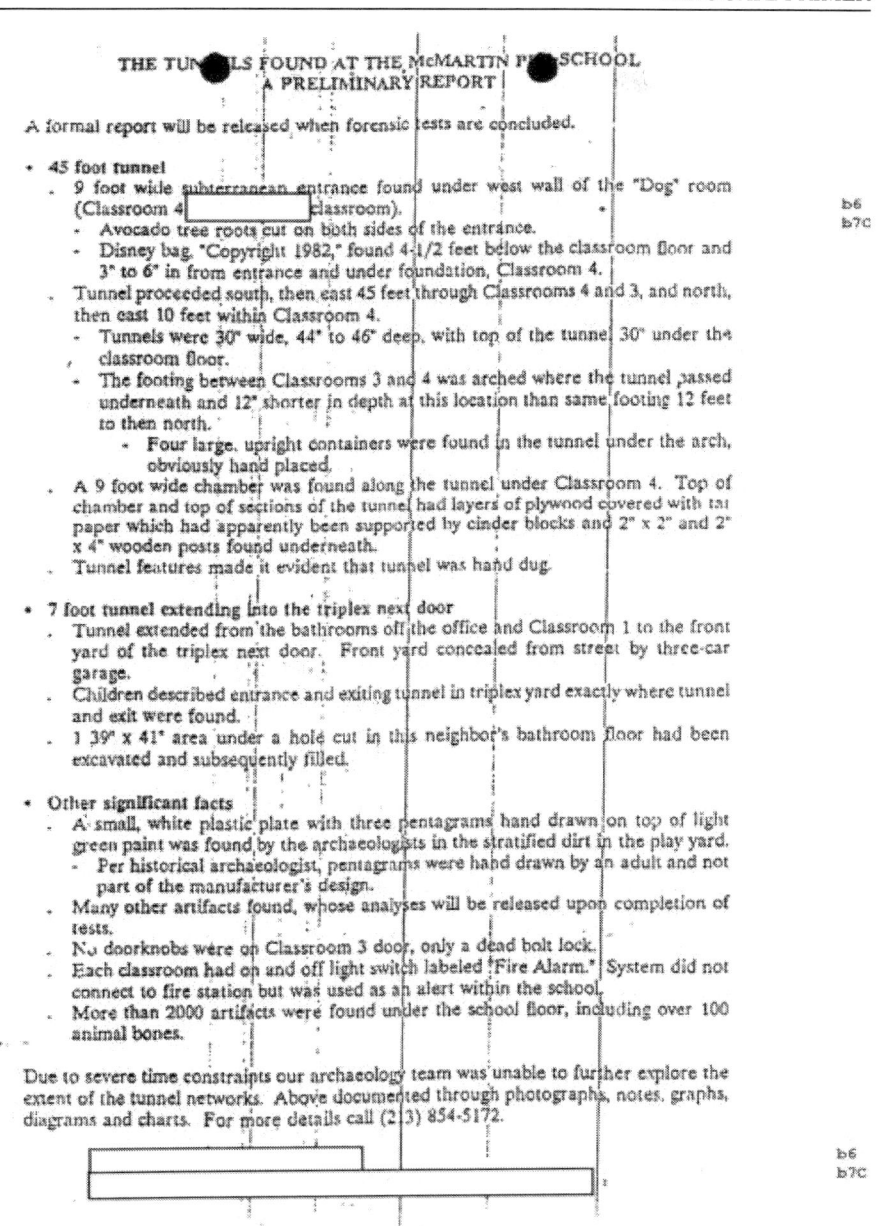

> THE TUNNELS FOUND AT THE McMARTIN PRESCHOOL
> A PRELIMINARY REPORT
>
> A formal report will be released when forensic tests are concluded.
>
> - **45 foot tunnel**
>   - 9 foot wide subterranean entrance found under west wall of the "Dog" room (Classroom 4 ▇▇▇ classroom).
>   - Avocado tree roots cut on both sides of the entrance.
>   - Disney bag. "Copyright 1982," found 4-1/2 feet below the classroom floor and 3" to 6" in from entrance and under foundation, Classroom 4.
>   - Tunnel proceeded south, then east 45 feet through Classrooms 4 and 3, and north, then east 10 feet within Classroom 4.
>   - Tunnels were 30" wide, 44" to 46" deep, with top of the tunnel 30" under the classroom floor.
>   - The footing between Classrooms 3 and 4 was arched where the tunnel passed underneath and 12" shorter in depth at this location than same footing 12 feet to then north.
>   - Four large, upright containers were found in the tunnel under the arch, obviously hand placed.
>   - A 9 foot wide chamber was found along the tunnel under Classroom 4. Top of chamber and top of sections of the tunnel had layers of plywood covered with tar paper which had apparently been supported by cinder blocks and 2" x 2" and 2" x 4" wooden posts found underneath.
>   - Tunnel features made it evident that tunnel was hand dug.
>
> - **7 foot tunnel extending into the triplex next door**
>   - Tunnel extended from the bathrooms off the office and Classroom 1 to the front yard of the triplex next door. Front yard concealed from street by three-car garage.
>   - Children described entrance and exiting tunnel in triplex yard exactly where tunnel and exit were found.
>   - 1 39" x 41" area under a hole cut in this neighbor's bathroom floor had been excavated and subsequently filled.
>
> - **Other significant facts**
>   - A small, white plastic plate with three pentagrams hand drawn on top of light green paint was found by the archaeologists in the stratified dirt in the play yard.
>   - Per historical archaeologist, pentagrams were hand drawn by an adult and not part of the manufacturer's design.
>   - Many other artifacts found, whose analyses will be released upon completion of tests.
>   - No doorknobs were on Classroom 3 door, only a dead bolt lock.
>   - Each classroom had on and off light switch labeled "Fire Alarm." System did not connect to fire station but was used as an alert within the school.
>   - More than 2000 artifacts were found under the school floor, including over 100 animal bones.
>
> Due to severe time constraints our archaeology team was unable to further explore the extent of the tunnel networks. Above documented through photographs, notes, graphs, diagrams and charts. For more details call (213) 854-5172.

New York Times's Retro Report released a short documentary on Dungeons and Dragons and the Satanic Panic. D&D and metal music were most certainly scapegoated during the period, but do the scapegoating and strawman arguments warrant throwing the baby with the bathwater? In 2014, *NYT* Retro Report examined "McMartin Preschool: Anatomy of a Panic." They spoke of how the case became a "national media obsession" that grew into a "panic around the country" fueled by the "unstinting belief this had happened."

Ironically the media blames themselves for the "sensational and lurid" coverage that fueled the Satanic Panic. The impact "lives on" with some still believing the stories of cases of child abuse which also feature "living creatures sacrificed" similar to what went on in the animal sacrifice photos uncovered in the Finders cult case. All in all, at McMartin 7 preschool teachers faced 300 counts of abuse. 7 other daycare centers in LA County, with several other communities, were to follow. This sudden outpouring in abuse stories was "not all it seemed" according to *NYT*.

The mother of the first complaining child "was psychotic" according to Debbie Nathan, investigative reporter and author of *Satan's Silence*. Kenneth Lanning shows up once again to "debunk" McMartin for *NYT* in 2014. Satanic abuse was "impossible to know with any degree of certainty" according to Lanning. Courts sealed the interviews with the children. The "underground tunnels" were often used to debunk the children's testimony, but as we've shown, the existence of those tunnels and evidence of animal bones and occult symbols were discovered. Just coming to terms with the phenomenon of child sexual abuse and how common it is is difficult. Another way the story was explained away was that "there should have been animal carcasses... they didn't have any of that."

To be fair, even the UCLA archaeologist Gary Stickel, who was hired by the families of the McMartin children, initially sided with the Buckeys until he came across the tunnels, animal bones and pentagram painting underground. This has been explained away by parents doing their own digging ignoring the fact that parents were allowed to volunteer helping at the guidance of Stickel. Another explanation is that the tunnels were simply a trash tunnel by a previous occupant of the property. Why one would need a tunnel from one building to another underground for your trash or why a pentagram would be found here is not explored by anyone who debunks McMartin.

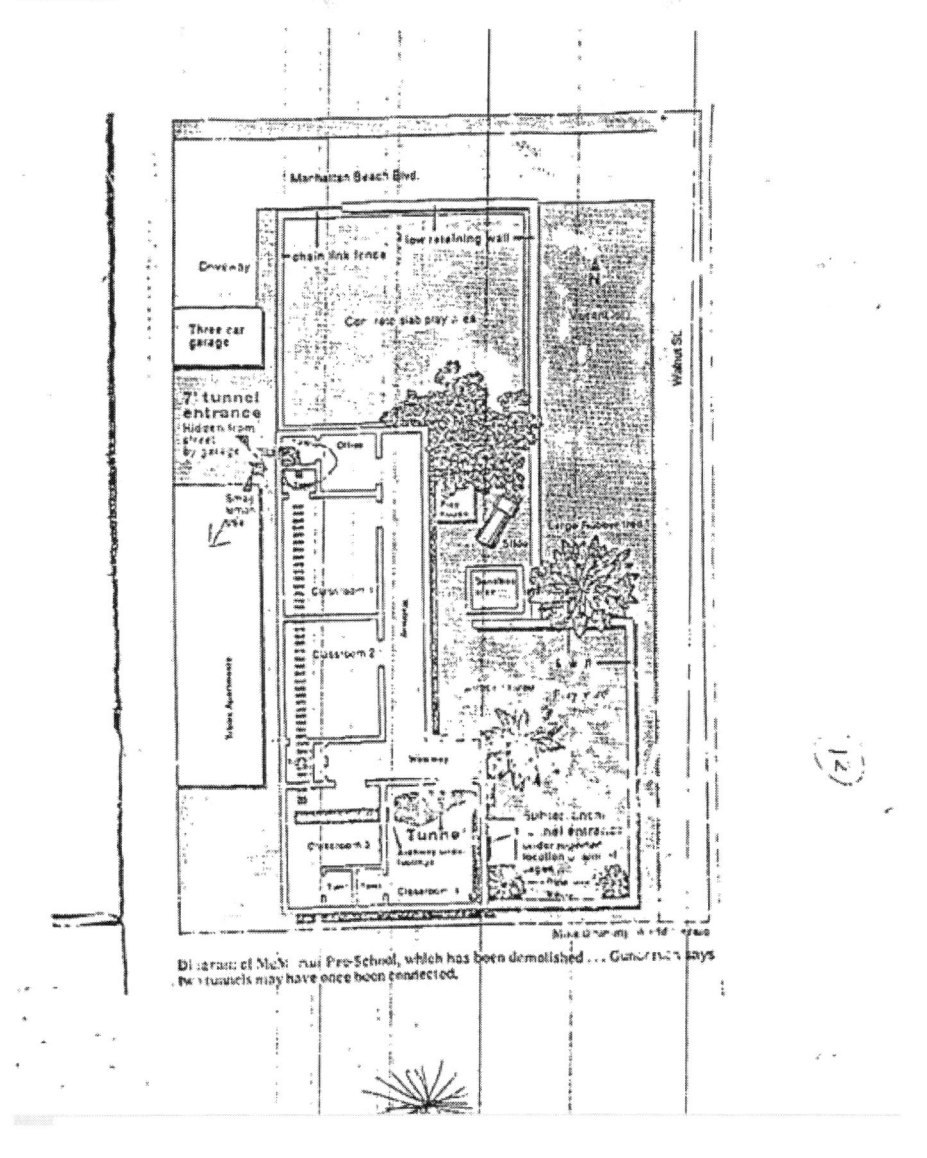

Diagram of McMartin Pre-School, which has been demolished ... Guner[?] says two tunnels may have once been connected.

Well of course this was in 2014 before the FBI released the McMartin tunnels diagram in the Finders Vault, including the animal bones and other things, so we can forgive the *New York Times* for their inaccuracy here.

According to *NYT*, "medical evidence supporting the prosecution's case couldn't be established with any certainty." Retro Report also points to how despite hundreds of children being interviewed only nine testified. This is true, but *NYT* neglects to mention that most of the children were not allowed to take the stand either because they were too young, while others that could have testified were not allowed on the stand because the statute of limitations expiration.

In addition to McMartin, there was a rash of other cases of preschool child abuse that popped up soon after including the Presidio scandal that seemed to implicate a former member of the Church of Satan and founder of the Temple of Set, Michael Aquino.

Gary Hambright, a Southern Baptist minister was accused of molesting dozens of children at San Francisco's Presidio Child Development Center. According to one FBI document, as many as 102 children may have fallen prey to Gary and/or others at the Army base daycare center. Hambright died of AIDS after which, the Army cited confidentiality laws that prevented them from discussing the number of children who may have been molested by Hambright being tested. Presidio spokesman Bob Mahoney claimed that "every kid that was brought in" was tested but "the victims and their families were all dispersed." Mahoney told the *San Jose Mercury News* he felt it would be "inappropriate" to comment on Hambright's death.

US Attorney Joseph Russoniello was the subject of a congressional subcommittee after deciding in 1988 not to prosecute the case. Despite, like at McMartin, the case being chalked up to hysteria and satanic panic three arson fires mysteriously occurred at the daycare center, and five of the children were diagnosed with sexually transmitted diseases. Contrary to internal military investigation, the ATF ruled that the fires were intentionally set.

In 1976 Paul Bynum was assigned to the Karen Klaas murder. Klaas was raped and murdered after dropping off her son at the McMartin preschool. Neighbors noted a "menacing stranger." In 1984, Gerald Klaas, her husband, was killed when he drove off a cliff.

Alex Constantine reports that the local rumor mill suggested the death may have had something to do with the McMartin case. Bynum was eventually forced out of the department via an order from the city manager putting him on permanent disability leave.

Bynum became a private investigator and was retained by the Buckey's defense attorney. The same day he was called to testify at Ray Buckey's trial a juror's home was burglarized and the testimony was rescheduled for the next day. "Neither side is going to like what I have to say," Bynum had claimed. This may have had something to do with the matter of some police records found in Buckey's home which were somehow lost later. There was also apparently a map that pointed out the location of turtle shells which seemed to corroborate children's claims of turtles being killed.

No one would hear Bynum's testimony, however. Former detective Paul Bynum, 39, would die when an "apparently self-inflicted" gunshot ended his life. A December 11, 1987, *Chronicle-Telegram* headline proclaimed "Another pre-school witness dead." This followed the death of Judy Johnson, the first mother to speak out about the alleged molestation. She died of alcohol toxicity just before she was to testify.

Another odd inconsistency is Peggy McMartin's claim to have only worked at the preschool for a short time despite payroll records showing she had been there for years. None of these inconsistencies are brought up as the CBC or Retro Report attempt to debunk the case as no more than Satanic Panic.

HOLLYWOOD, POP CULTURE AND THE CULTURED PEDOPHILES

Does the #MeToo movement leave children behind? It seems so.

"I accidentally worked with a pedophile," Rose McGowan said on *The View*, "and I bet you have too."

"I will say," she went on, "that probably everyone has accidentally worked with a pedophile, and I don't take joy in that."

This was from Rose McGowan after Justin Timberlake rebuffed her for shaming him for working with Woody Allen by bringing up her work with convicted child molester and child pornographer Victor Salva. Victor Salva was convicted of raping a 12-year-old boy who starred in one of his first films as well as filming the abuse itself to add to his collection.

McGowan has defended her work with Salva saying she "didn't know" about his past. That's a statement that's hard to defend, however. In an interview with the LGBT magazine *The Advocate* she mentioned feeling somewhat awkward when Salva told her he "didn't relate to women well." The journalist at *The Advocate* expounded, "Well, Salva is a registered sex offender, which might account for some awkwardness." Rose's reply? "Yeah, I still don't really understand the whole story or history there, and I'd rather not, because it's not really my business. But he's an incredibly sweet and gentle man, lovely to his crew, and a very hard worker."

That's right, the mother of the #rosearmy decided she'd rather turn her head to child abuse. Evidently sexual harassment and assault are only issues when it's millionaire adults being victimized in

Rose's book. Sadly though, with all the talk of Hollywood's sexual excesses, improprieties, harassment, assaults, and abuses one thing that is not mentioned often is the dark, pedophile underworld that Rose even half admits. As for how much of an accident it was, sounds like she intentionally turned her head like so many people do when they don't want to see something too horrible to comprehend.

Salva's name may or may not ring any bells but even for folks who aren't horror fanatics you've likely heard of a few of his films. If you're a fan of horror flicks, you've almost certainly seen, or at least heard of the *Jeepers Creepers* series. With actors and directors being canceled for sexual harassment and offensive tweets, for some reason films like *Jeepers Creepers 3* can be made and a multiple times accused child abuser like Bryan Singer was even honored with an Oscar award.

If you weren't already familiar with Victor Salva, the writer-director, you'll most likely be shocked to find out that Salva is a convicted child molester and child pornographer. After raping a 12-year-old boy on the set of his first film *Clownhouse*, he was sentenced to 3 years, of which he spent less than a year and a half in prison. Amazing what money can do for you, huh? And that's what it comes down to.

Speaking of money, if the idea of dropping coins in the pocket of a literal child rapist doesn't seem exceedingly palatable, then please make sure you do not watch movies like *Clownhouse*, *Powder* and the *Jeepers Creepers* series. Nathan Forest Winters will never act again. The 12-year-old boy who was kept behind on the set to make a different sort of movie for Victor Salva's sick pleasures.

Winters himself has pleaded:

"Please don't spend your money on this movie. It would just go to line the pockets of this child molester. I needed to face this. I've lived through years and years and years of pain and trauma. I'm being healed daily. It's unreal the amount of stuff that's built up all these years that's starting to be released. But it doesn't work like, 'Boom! – I'm OK now.'"

It's amazing that with all the fury at serial abusers like Weinstein, a monster like Salva can go literally unnoticed. For child and adult victims of abuse, this is a frightening prospect, the thought that a monster like this could run free. Who needs cinematic villains like Freddie Krueger when real life Creepers like Victor are offered millions for indulging their sick fantasies on the silver screen.

The fact that Disney would hire a convicted child molester is surprising (if you're not familiar with how Disney really works).

Consider the fact that the Disney movie, written and directed by Victor the pederast, had its opening picketed by Winters to no avail is a shameful fact and enough for me to spurn the family company entirely. This especially shouldn't be surprising considering Bella Thorne, a Disney channel kid all grown up now, admitted multiple of her bosses and coworkers at Disney were aware that she was being abused and did absolutely nothing to stop it.

Of course why would the family company care? After Nickelodeon fired Brian Peck for sexually assaulting a child under 14, Disney thought it would be a bright idea to hire him to work on the Suite Life with Zach and Cody. Sweet life for a child molester certainly. Like a kid in a candy store or a pedophile at an amusement park.

Ezel Channel was also convicted of molesting a child while at Nickelodeon. Brian Peck, who ran a "comedy boot camp" with Dan Schneider, worked on *All That* and was convicted of raping a child on set. Then there's Marty Weiss, former manager scout whose clients worked on shows like *iCarly*, also convicted of raping a client. Jason M. Handy, another offender was a production assistant on *All That* and *The Amanda Show*.

This is by no means a one-off, remember when Corey Feldman bravely admitted that he was "passed around" like a party favor by powerful Hollywood types? Barbara Walters scolded him saying he was "damaging an industry." Damaging an industry? An industry of child exploiters and abusers should be disparaged and damaged at every step.

This is nothing new either. Shirley Temple starred in a series known as "Baby Burlesque" films when she was barely older than a toddler. A notable example from the '70s would be Todd Bridges.

Todd Bridges was especially uncomfortable while filming the "very special episode" of Diff'rent Strokes in which a pedophile is grooming Gary Coleman. The reason for this (apart from the laugh track going off at some disturbingly inappropriate moments) is that he went through a similar situation and, once again, it was major Hollywood players responsible for the abuse.

Molly Ringwald, came out after the #MeToo scandal broke as well:

"When I was thirteen, a fifty-year-old crew member told me that he would teach me to dance, and then proceeded to push against me with an erection. At fourteen, a married film director stuck his tongue in my mouth on set. At a time when I was trying to figure out what it meant to become a sexually viable young woman, at every turn some older guy tried to help speed up the process."

A member of the Latin boy band Menudo admits that he was molested decades ago as a child multiple times and at least a couple of those times it was "friends of friends" of the execs. Corey Haim was 11-years-old when an older man on set took him aside to have sex. He told the young Haim it was "what all the guys do." Corey Feldman talked to ABC News about the situation: "I can tell you the number one problem was and is and always will be pedophilia. It's all done under the radar. It's the big secret. I was surrounded by them when I was 14-years-old. Literally. They were everywhere, like vultures." As mentioned earlier, Barbara Walters responded chastising him for condemning the Hollywood industry.

Former child star James Van Der Beek of the teen soap opera Dawson's Creek talked about his experiences being assaulted by "older, powerful men" as well. Jeannette McCurdy all but came out about her experiences with Dan Schneider. "Look at me, look what you've done to me, I know you're watching my vine Dan Schneider."

Dan Schneider would abruptly part ways with Nickelodeon. In addition to being one of their top writers and producers for many years, Schneider had a reputation of having a bit of a temper and due to some of his tweets, his obsession with feet, certain sequences he recorded that never appeared in the shows and his being targeted by ex-stars like Jeanette McCurdy, many believed him to be a serial child exploiter. From soliciting pictures of feet from children through the official Sam and Cat television show Twitter account to "parent-free" pool parties hosted by Dan, there is enough to give one pause.

Interestingly enough, not many major venues brought up this issue apart from Deadline.com and Jezebel. The website Revenge of the Cis had talked with someone who claimed to have left one of Schneider's "grooming camps." For a time *PEOPLE, AOL, Entertainment, The Hollywood Reporter* and *Bustle* showed some interest in the story but none decided to speak with the witness.

That said, within days *Ren and Stimpy* creator Jon Kricfalusi had been called out for allegedly grooming two young girls who spoke with *Buzzfeed* news. One of the two women who came forward to Buzzfeed, Robyn Byrd says she began to write Kricfalusi when she was just 14. She expressed her interest in becoming an animator and he offered to mentor her. By the time she was 16, he had flown her to Los Angeles. While she was there she relates how he touched her genitals through her pajamas. By the Summer of 1997, she was living with him and working as an intern for his animation studio, Spumco. She considered the relationship with the *Ren and Stimpy* creator (15 years her senior) a romantic entanglement that was often turbulent. She moved out permanently in 2002 and found she couldn't draw anymore as she associated the act with Kricfalusi.

There have even been allegations of children's media assisting in the "grooming" process. I'd never heard of this movie *Show Dogs*. I don't pay a lot of attention to the latest on television or coming out of Hollywood generally, but a review of this movie had me seriously disturbed. I honestly can't imagine what it would be like taking children to see the film, how awkward it would be trying to explain some incredibly unnecessary material.

The movie *Show Dogs* features a talking police dog (voiced by former rapper Ludacris) who is working with a human partner, Frank (Will Arnett). Frank and Max are trying to bust up a kidnapping ring and rescue a baby panda and their best bet is to infiltrate a dog show competition. At first it's just typical children's entertainment, but evidently, there's a bit of... weirdness that crops up as well.

At one point, Max the police dog has to learn how to be inspected by the judges. The competition dogs (who equate perhaps to Hollywood royalty or the elite in general) are not only glamorous but also nonchalant about certain aspects of the dog show lifestyle, unlike Max who is a "street smart" New York dog.

An entire subplot in the film is dedicated to preparing Max for the genital inspection portion of the show. Frank and a former dog show champion try to help acclimate Max, but it makes him uncomfortable, so he's told to go to his "zen place" when it's happening. The reviewer of the film was apparently a child abuse victim and can surely vouch for the dissociation that often occurs in situations of repeat child abuse. Max's plight nearly mirrors that of a child being groomed.

Then there's the moral of the story. To fit in with the more glamorous show dogs as well as to "save the day" Max must allow himself to be molested and learn to just get used to it by dissociating and retreating to his happy place. I haven't seen this movie (and after the description, I am certain never to suggest it to anyone with children) but the reviewer shared their opinion of the resolution to the quasi-grooming sub-plot.

"The day of the finals come, and if Max doesn't let his private parts be touched, he may lose the competition and any hope of finding the kidnapped panda. It all rests on his ability to let someone touch his private parts. The judge's hands slowly reach behind Max and he goes to his 'zen place.' He's flying through the sky, dancing with his partner, there are fireworks and flowers-everything is great-all while someone is touching his private parts."

With the #MeToo movement and all the talk of sexual predators in Hollywood, I couldn't help but think this message, that is blatantly in the open for adults to see, but above a child's understanding, is meant to groom children to be open to having people touch their privates, even though they don't want it. It gives them the idea of a "zen place" to go to mentally when they are touched.

A similar, more recent situation involved a Troll's World Tour doll that had several pre-recorded messages when you squeezed its belly.

Inexplicably, the doll would make moaning noises if you pressed a button in the genital region. As with the previously mentioned film, the doll was pulled and an apology, sans explanation, ensued.

A glaring indictment of being found out is the fact that after the outrage the scene and toy respectively were pulled. Why would anyone write a scene for children or design a toy like this? Your guess is as good as mine. Perhaps these things just accidentally happen, perhaps not.

The #MeToo movement shook up Hollywood and numerous abuses were exposed but very little of Hollywood's dark secrets involving children were revealed.

Roseanne was recently fired from her own show for a controversial tweet. Evidently, her Ambien influenced tweet was considered both racist and Islamophobic and that's just not the kind of thing that ABC and Disney want to align themselves with. It would seem to be a matter of principles and standards, but taking a look at some people currently and previously involved with Disney/ABC it seems likely it was more of a public relations band-aid. James Gunn was also ousted for a time from directing Marvel movies for a time due to a series of disturbing "jokes" about pedophilia, the same sort that Patton Oswalt and several other comedians have made. Whether they hide something more nefarious is hard to tell as comedy often intentionally tackles dark topics.

Disney, ABC, and Nickelodeon have a few things in common. Besides being known for family entertainment, they have a history of hiring convicted pedophiles and sexual predators. Brian Peck, for instance, was convicted in 2004 of two counts of sexual abuse of an underage star who worked with him at Nickelodeon. Peck faced multiple charges but ended up convicted on one count of a lewd act against a child and one count of oral copulation of a person under 16. Peck admitted to his wrongdoing.

Peck had a history of working with children's entertainment. After being released he was hired, once again, to work on a children's show, Disney's Yay, Me! and The Suite Life of Zack & Cody. Victor Salva is another convicted child molester who was also accused of creating child pornography from the abuse he inflicted on the young boy he had been molesting for nearly five years. Salva is responsible for the movie *Powder* which was released by Disney owned Caravan Pictures. When *Powder* first came out, Salva's victim, Nathan Forrest Winters protested the film's release but there wasn't much of an effect considering the film grossed $31 million (over three times the estimated budget to make the movie).

Here's what *LA Times* had to say in 1995 when *Powder* became a breakout hit for the man who has released the third movie in the popular *Jeepers Creepers* franchise:

"As controversy swirled around filmmaker Victor Salva, who pleaded guilty in 1988 to molesting a boy on the set of his low-budget picture *Clownhouse*, Salva's agent said that a good showing at the box office may salvage the 37-year-old director's career."

Joel Iwataki is another example of a child predator who, unlike Roseanne, evidently fits the mold of family friendly in Disney's opinion. Iwataki has worked on multiple Disney projects most recently *Incredibles 2* and *Coco*. Iwataki is a registered sex offender convicted of lewd or lascivious acts with a child under 14 years of age. If you look up Iwataki's name you'll first see he's an Emmy award winner who worked on 150 films. His Google featured snippet leaves out any details of his history of sexual abuse of a minor.

ABC and Disney have a reputation to protect as a family-oriented studio, but when it comes down to it, are they really concerned with anything more than the blowback they might receive? Imagine if people cared as much about the fact that Disney/ABC was employing convicted child rapists as they were with coarse opinions shared through social media.

Despite all the talk of witch hunts, there are occasions where these dark topics bleed over into popular media. The series Stranger Things seems to allude to MK-Ultra and Project Stargate experiments. Then there's True Detective. I watched the first season of True Detective back in 2013 and remembered noticing the symbol. Though it came to the forefront after Pizzagate became a household name, information about the multiple symbols used by pedophiles to identify themselves secretly have been available online at least since the early 2000's when I started seriously researching institutional pedophilia.

In addition to the Franklin Cover-Up (which potentially embroiled George Bush and others in a prostitution scandal that hearkened back to the Cleveland Street Scandal of turn of 1890's England) True Detective spins stories based on details from the case of the Hosanna Church of Louisiana which involved child abuse, satanism and rituals involving sacrifices and cat blood.

The True Detective anthology series came back. There were doubts about the show being renewed after the critics panned season 2. Season 3 returned to the topic of people in power connected to child trafficking, Satanism and the cover-ups that can ensue as a result.

The District Attorney who prosecuted the case said it was never anything about satanism, discounting claims of babies being "dedicated" to Satan and blood rituals.

Of course, officially the DA is right. DA Scott Perrilloux attested that the case "had nothing to do with a church or a cult or any sort of high-pressure situation." Despite what the pastor/leader of the alleged cult told the Parish Sheriff when he turned himself in, the "Satanic" angle is dismissed. The boys themselves later recanted their claims of any Satanic abuse as well, and the story was relegated to a case of later Satanic Panic. Louis Lamonica would be the second of the seven on trial for child abuse and molestation from the Hosanna church in Pontachoula, Louisiana.

The Satanic Panic was a witch hunt as Paul Campos wrote in *The Week* in March of 2014, True Detective, with its conspicuous usage of known pedophile trafficking gang symbols, was spreading "dangerous lies." The article immediately draws parallels between the show and D.W. Griffith's *The Birth of a Nation* which glorified the South and praised the Ku Klux Klan as protectors of Dixie in the era of Reconstruction. According to Campos, True Detectives is presenting a "massive distortion of the historical truth" to broadcast its "noxious lies about the past into art."

If you search McMartin or Presidio (or other famous cases involving our aforementioned keywords), you'll see many a work has been published decrying the Satanic Panic. And, hey, demonizing Dungeons and Dragons and karate as equivalent to devil worship is kind of extreme in my opinion, but there may have been more to it in a few cases.

We've mentioned the case of The Finders cult and their implication in child abuse, molestation, trafficking and rituals involving animal abuse and desecration several times. After the case left the local police department and Customs and Border Patrol became involved due to evidence of international child trafficking it literally became a federal case. At this time, none other than the Central Intelligence Agency decided to put the lid on the whole thing by declaring the whole affair "an internal matter."

Very likely several, possibly most, of the purported cases of Satanic Ritual Abuse are embellished or, indeed, witch hunts. It's impossible to know how many true cases of extreme and sadistic sexual abuse of persons, sometimes or often children, for evil, occultic purposes there are, but the evidence left over from The Finders is ample enough to prove a Black Swan, the exception that disproves the rule.

It's obvious that even in some of the articles that speak glowingly of the show, there's a sort of questioning of "but what is he trying to say, where is he going with this?" *Vanity Fair* even makes sure to mention the show is a hit with "online conspiracy theorists." In the era of "the Qanon bomber" and Edgar Maddison Welch, the "Pizzagate Shooter" the idea of questioning the narrative of official news and history is viewed as more than subversive, potentially dangerous and a likely benchmark for detecting radicalism or a terrorist in the making.

Season 2, as mentioned, was critically panned and performed poorly in ratings. It also was the only of the three that didn't deal directly with (possibly ritual) abuse and murder as central to the plot. I have my own theories on why season 2 strayed from the ranch and nearly ended the franchise.

In episode 2 of season 3 there's even a mention of the Franklin Scandal and the crooked spiral that came to some mainstream attention when Wikileaks released details about symbols related to organized child abuse and trafficking as per the FBI.

Jacob Wetterling's 1988 abduction is conflated with that of the West Memphis Three. Meanwhile, even the story of the boys on the tracks is referenced. Though the case of the death of two young boys was initially ruled an accident, chalked up to smoking marijuana and falling asleep on train tracks, stab wounds, and other inconsistencies raised alarm bells.

The wife of one of the main characters in season 3 is a teacher turned author. She likely is meant to represent Mara Leveritt who wrote *Boys On The Tracks: A Mother's Crusade For Justice* as well as reporting on the West Memphis Three story.

The Clintons' purported connection to drug dealing may also have been slyly referenced in the second episode as well. A woman exclaims that there's "heroin in Arkansas." At the time the show takes place, Bill Clinton was governor of Arkansas and, like George H.W. Bush, has been implicated in drug running by CIA-connected pilot Barry Seal through Mena, Arkansas.

I've also got my own opinions on what the earlier drafts of the movie, *Mena* was like before Tom Cruise nearly died in the helicopter stunt and they changed the name to *American Made*. I've got a feeling that the earlier drafts of season 2 of True Detective might have been a bit more interesting as well.

It is notable that with all this hullabaloo about the behind the scenes bacchanalia in Hollywood with Weinsteins and their ilk having their way with any woman who wants a career, the Dan Schneiders of the world squeak by considering the fact that it is literally *An Open Secret*. Incidentally, *An Open Secret* is the name of an award winning documentary that outed Digital Entertainment Network (DEN) and their monetized grooming and abuse of several young boys who were attempting to break into the world of child acting. I highly recommend the documentary to those who are interested in learning more about Hollywood's culture of child abuse.

Speaking of open secrets, the stories related to Dan Schneider were pretty much an open secret for years. The rumors have gotten louder as of late and with the #MeToo and #TimesUp campaigns still in swing, I was amazed no lids had yet been blown off.

Charlie Sheen was accused by his ex-wife of harboring child pornography which would seem to corroborate Cory Feldman's claims Sheen was one of his and Haim's abusers.

When I heard the news that Nickelodeon had "finally parted ways" with the biggest writer, director and producer they've had in a quarter of a century straight out of the blue, I thought to myself, here it is. It's beginning. It's finally happening. The rumors resurfaced with a vengeance when Jamie Lynn Spears was absent at the Zoey 101 cast reunion Schneider attended.

It's mostly circumstantial still, of course, there's his weird Twitter feed where he's constantly talking about the feet of the young girls who star in his shows. The stories of pool parties without parental supervision, backstage footage where he sits in hot tubs with the likes of Amanda Bynes.

Then there are the weird subtextually sexual scenes that only make it as far as the cutting room floor (and perhaps Schneider's own personal collection). Like one featuring Ariana Grande squeezing a potato near her mouth and groaning, "Ugggh, give up the juice."

Speaking of Amanda Bynes, there are rumors that her unhinged behavior may be, in part, seated in years of abuse at the hands of Dan and those like him. Jeanette McCurdy (whose toes Dan has tweeted about multiple times) is made up in a similar fashion to Bynes in a vine that was entitled #DanSchneider. Jeanette also posted a vine with herself naked in a bathtub showing off bruises shortly before the series of Dan Schneider vines.

There are all those overly handsy photos of Dan with his preteen and barely pubescent starlets. All that in addition to the backstage videos in a hot tub with Amanda Bynes and the stories of unchaperoned pool parties then thousands of deleted tweets overnight after he was ejected from Nickelodeon. Really makes you think.

Once again, for the most part, it's just some unnerving and creepy things that have unsettled more and more people for years, but the rumors just kept becoming more and more widespread and had been circling for years. It's a case of guilt by association but there's the fact that he was friends and colleagues with Brian Peck.

An article from the *LA Times* from 2002 was literally entitled "Groomed to Be All That," about the "comedy boot camp" that child sex offender Peck and Schneider worked where they "discovered" Amanda Bynes. Peck had sex with a Nickelodeon star who is not named and then there's Jason Michael Handy, again, another Nickelodeon predator. James Murphy a convicted sex offender worked at Nickelodeon until it was discovered he was a convicted sex offender and pedophile. But once again, this is just guilt by association (by the forkloads) and circumstantial evidence (by the truckloads).

But along with all his success, for years Schneider had been under a cloud of suspicion over the treatment of some younger stars of his shows. Among things that have raised eyebrows are his tweeted photos of the toes of his young female stars. Additionally, there have been issues with bloated budgets and long production days on Schneider's shows.

Shortly after his being let go a source close to him spoke to the media about him:

"Schneider has had well-documented temper issues for years. I hear there was a flareup last week during a meeting he had with Nickelodeon executives where they indicated to him that Game Shakers was not getting renewed for a fourth season. Sources say that Schneider's reaction was, at least in part, due to the fact that Game Shakers was about to wrap production on its third season the following day with a cliffhanger season finale, which would leave fans without closure.

I hear at the meeting Schneider also was told that, with his other Nick comedy, Henry Danger, on hiatus, another show (I hear it's Austin & Ally creators Kevin Kopelow and Heath Seifert's new Nick series, Cousins for Life), would move into the production space in the Nickelodeon-owned Burbank studios which has housed Schneider's series exclusively for the past few years. Sources say that Schneider objected to the prospect of having to share the office and production space with the non-Bakery show."

There is even behind the scenes footage that amps up the creep factor. "Did you say nice things about me? Cuz I will taze her." Dan says to a slightly creeped out Miranda Cosgrove after which the ABC cameraman on the scene disapprovingly answers, "That's gonna get on TV. That is gonna get on TV."

Another child star, Miley Cyrus at 15 was posing for "sexy" photographs in *Vanity Fair* in 2008... topless under a sheet alongside her father, failed country music star, Billy Ray Cyrus.

Pedophilia and child sexualization in Hollywood is nothing new. The normalization of "intergenerational sex" as the euphemism goes has gone on for decades. Harvard publication *The Crimson's* "Politics, Pederasty and Consciousness" mentions Allen Ginsberg, the renowned Beatnik poet. In the interview Ginsberg admits to the difficulties facing the aging pedophile:

"As I get older, having very specialized sexual tastes, it gets harder to make out... I like young boys. Why? Well, I'm not a young teenager. I'd have more chance at making out with younger guys if I were younger, dewier, dewy-limbed."

An essay from *The Poem that Changed America: "Howl" Fifty Years Later*, describes Ginsberg's position on pedophilia, making it a form of Thoreauvian dissent like his use of mind-expanding drugs or getting the f-word printed in books of literature:

"For Ginsberg, pederasty was just another one of his happy crimes."

Ginsberg made headlines after receiving a 1 million dollar grant from Stanford. The man who had earned the ire of the establishment for acting as a spokesman for psychedelics, the anti-war movement, the antinuclear movement and tirelessly opposing censorship. This time it was his unabashed support of the North American Man-Boy Love Association (NAMBLA) that caused such an upset.

Ginsberg and Burroughs were open about their dalliances with young men and boys. At the spark of the sexual revolution that was inspired in part by the work of Alfred Kinsey and Masters & Johnson, figures like Allen Ginsberg challenged the normative views of sexuality that dominated 1950s America. Some good came of this, for instance, the civil rights struggle for equality homosexuals strived for. Burroughs and Ginsberg are towering figures among the Beatniks and any top ten list of 20th century American poets is sure to feature Allen but striving for equality for pedophiles is a bridge too far for most people regardless of how progressive they view themselves.

Another point that should be made is that the sex, drugs and rock 'n roll generation brought a generation of child groupies to the fore. In a post-MeToo world, the stories of Jimmy Page kidnapping a barely pubescent girl

and keeping her hidden from her parents is viewed in a different light.

Chuck Klosterman described Page's "legendary appetite for jailbait" in a *Spin* article about the sleaziest of all rock and rollers. The Aleister Crowley loving Page sounded unrepentant and downright Thelemic in a 1985 interview in which he bragged, "I've never done anything a person didn't want. I've done everything you've ever heard."

Incidentally, Page would dump Lori Mattix when she apparently aged out at 16 David Bowie also admitted to affairs with 13 and 14-year old groupies. Steven Tyler didn't raise his own daughter Liv because he was too busy impregnating his adopted teenage daughter. Tyler now operates a charity for abused young women.

In Hollywood, the most famous examples are likely Kevin Spacey and Woody Allen. Woody is generally blasted for his relationship with Mia Farrow's adopted daughter Soon-Yi. He was said by many to have groomed her for years before their relationship. More shocking are the claims that he molested his adopted daughter Dylan Farrow at age 7.

Meghan Kane, staff writer with *The Progressive Teen* writes about the topic of rock and roll artists and underage girls in "Jail Bait: The Dark Relationship between Rock 'n' Roll and Pedophilia." Kane points out that many of these artists "seem to be very straightforward when singing about sex crimes, coming right out and saying what they mean without beating around the bush."

Ted Nugent's song *Jailbait* with its lyrics of "Well, I don't care if you're just thirteen" or Kiss' "Christine Sixteen" are just a couple examples of grown men flaunting sex with underage girls. To prove it wasn't all talk, the Nuge took the Steven Tyler approach by becoming the legal guardian of a 17-year-old Hawaiian girl so he could have sex with her without repercussions.

"I don't usually say things like this, but when I saw you coming out of school that day, that day I knew, I knew, I've got to have you! I've got to have you!" Kiss sing blatantly about an, apparently out of character, pick-up of a school-aged girl.

In addition to mentioning Tyler forcing his adopted ward to have an abortion, Kane mentions Bill Wyman's relationship with a 13-year-old girl. This was nothing new by the way. Jerry Lee Lewis' relationship with his 13-year-old cousin hearkens back to Edgar Allen Poe's forbidden familial love with his own 13-year-old cousin.

According to some accounts even the King of Rock 'n roll, Elvis Presley himself, was known to pick up girls as young as 14. Priscilla Presley herself was only 14 when she met Elvis. Presley, already a rock star of great acclaim at the time, had previously taken a 15-year-old girl to her Junior Prom.

The King of Pop, Michael Jackson, was abused as a child himself. In turn, he seems to have been somewhat stunted emotionally. As a result, he was open about how he felt it was perfectly fine and normal to invite prepubescent boys for sleepovers and enjoy his Neverland ranch. The very name evoking the lost boys who never grow up in J.M. Barrie's *Peter Pan*.

Despite the incredible aftershocks of the #MeToo and Epstein scandals, still, the idea of powerful people abusing children on a wide scale was apparently too horrific for most people to want to believe. Before Adam Parfrey died, I remember him alluding a couple of times in correspondence and on social media to squeaky clean Tom Hanks having some dark secrets (though he never went into detail regarding exactly what those might be). As far as "guardian of gossip," Parfrey was the Gen X answer to Kenneth Anger, author of *Hollywood Babylon*. Anger's volume, by the way, reveals how Charlie Chaplin too was a fan of girls under 14 among other extremes and excesses of the golden age of Hollywood royalty. Statutory rapist Errol Flynn slid by without so much as hardly skinning his nose. The idiom "in like Flynn" refers to his legendary prowess at seduction of girls of various ages.

Before his untimely death in 2019, Parfrey was privy to much of the juiciest rumors and whispers of gossip in the world of pop culture and Hollywood. As "the most dangerous publisher in America" as he was often referred, he rarely steered clear from speaking his mind either. Long before the terms pedogate or pizzagate were common or the stories of Nickelodeon and Disney serially hiring child abusers, Parfrey was out there outing Pedowood.

In 1993, Parfrey contributed an article to Jim Goad's controversial *Answer Me!* magazine entitled "Pederastic Park." As it turns out the rumors of Steven Spielberg's "overweening fascination with child actors" as Parfrey puts it, are nothing new. Parfrey makes sure to protect himself by pointing out that though he's just relating the murmurs he has heard over the years "the fact that this rumor exists at all confirms an underlying unease over the presumably innocent entertainments created by Hollywood's oldest Wunderkind."

In 1993 Spielberg was already a household name and was busy striking gold with the first installment in the *Jurassic Park* franchise. Parfrey was more concerned with the "failed" Robin Williams vehicle *Hook*. A retelling of a story by, rumored pedophile and classic children's author, J.M. Barrie.

Hook, Parfrey noted, "reveals components of the auteur's personality that have parents wondering about the movie's appropriateness for kids." Well, gee whiz, what could be more wholesome than a story about a "boy forever" whose first name is a euphemism for male genitalia and last name is a well-known god of lust who spends all his time being chased after by an obsessive, much older man?

In the 1993 article, Parfrey goes on to explain how *Hook* was "the culmination of over a decade of false starts in bringing J.M. Barrie's *Peter Pan* to the screen. At first, Spielberg was reportedly considering a live-action redo of the Disney animated feature, starring Michael Jackson as the perpetual pre-pube."

Parfrey also touches on how timely the concept piece was considering how it fits in perfectly with the "recovery metaphysics" of 90s Hollywood. A place where "continual cocaine-and-Quaalude concatenations" are replaced by spirit journeys, New Age therapies, and a quest to "liberate the inner child." A main goal of the "Me Generation" it seems was to feed the child (and childishness) of the yuppie class. Foundations like Esalen have made hundreds of millions from the privileged class. Trading countless bundles of cold, hard cash so that the "poor" upper class can learn about the dangers of materialism.

Parfrey pulls no punches even at the time of Spielberg's peak:

"Asking Steven Spielberg to liberate his inner child would be akin to asking a serial murderer to actualize his anger. By his own admission, Stevie has experienced little in the way of adulthood outside of his overprotective upbringing and the adulatory, toadying fantasy land of Hollywood. Bradshaw's 'inner child' therapy is a mere baby-step away from the Diaper Pail Fraternity, a Sausalito-based group for grown men who revert to incontinent fantasy, where surrogate mommies exclaim and coo as they wipe the kinky kid-fetishists' dirty behinds."

Parfrey also name drops "ex-drunk" John Bradshaw and former Spielberg producer Julia Phillips while referring to "workshops" where infantilized Hollywood types rock and cradle each other with lullaby music playing in the background.

Spielberg's Pan fantasy was released "at the crest of the child-abuse wave" during a time when media was saturated with stories of molestation, incest, and numerous cases of institutional pedophilia and even what appeared to be potential ritual abuse. The film, via its poster "transferred any possible pedophilic overtones from Spielberg himself (the auteur) to the classically pederastic fantasy figure of Captain Hook."

Parfrey also managed to track down a writer for the NAMBLA Bulletin, L. Martin whose primary responsibilities included documenting "the doings of such Hollywood chickens as Macauley Culkin, known affectionately in the bulletin as 'Mac.'"

NAMBLA writer Martin noted that "Spielberg is known for his interest in young boys, certainly. A lot of the members have been talking about *Hook,* telling me how much they enjoyed it." A NAMBLA spokesman however invoked the child molester's equivalent of the Glomar response and "refused to confirm or deny" any potential membership but did point out the existence of Paedo Alert News (known as P.A.N.) which could be a double entendre referring to the Barrie classic and the Greek, satyr God of lust.

There is even some conjecture on Parfrey's part at Amblin being a play on NAMBLA. The NAMBLA name game seems to result in some interesting coincidences. Lambda Literary and the Lambda Book Report and the Lambda Rising bookstore which carried NAMBLA's bulletin are all members of the "Lambda family." Technically unrelated to Lambda Legal, but that group has defended NAMBLA as being "obnoxious" but certainly not pedophiles or members of a sex ring despite multiple cases of members of NAMBLA coordinating to either share child pornography, organize illegal sex tourism visits or kidnap and rape minors.

If you don't feel like watching Spielberg ever again, I highly recommend reading the entire article in which Parfrey deconstructs several of Spielberg's films which will likely ensure you swear off his movies for good. As Parfrey notes, "perhaps the most perverse aspect of Steven Spielberg's work is its obsessive posture of sentimental innocence." This was around the same time theories of subliminal sexual messages in Disney movies began. Within years, sexualization of preteens and teens such as Lindsay Lohan and Miley Cyrus would become a sort of constant backdrop to the developing minds of many young children.

R. Kelly was known to have groomed Aaliyah professionally and sexually, and caught on video urinating on a girl who was 15 or under. Despite all this being fairly public knowledge, until the spate of interest in the past few years R. Kelly floated along building his harem of often underage girls.

Public broadcasting channel KQED asks why Americans can't come to terms with Gary Glitter. His song "Rock & Roll Part 2" is one of the most widely played songs at any sporting event that isn't by the band Queen. It also appeared in the movie *Joker*. The song seems to have not suffered from Glitter's shattered reputation.

Glitter was placed on Britain's sex offender registry and forced to spend four months in prison after 4,000 child sexual exploitation images, some of children 6 or younger, were found on his computer. He fled for Cambodia until he was deported for sex tourism and later arrested by Vietnamese police after multiple incidents involving children as young as 10 or 11. He would serve three years in prison in Vietnam and was barred from 19 countries including Philippines, Cuba, Cambodia and Thailand. In 2008 he was finally deported to the UK.

Glitter, who was a friend of Jimmy Savile and apparently shared the same proclivities, was netted as part of Operation Yewtree. Sex abuse of children from 8 to 15 earned him a 16 year sentence. Though he apparently sold the rights to "Rock & Roll Part 2", he still earns money via "usually outspoken feminist" Joan Jett and others licensing his music to cover it:

"Jett has kept that song alive and, according to a 2008 report in *The Telegraph*, Glitter has profited. After Hewlett Packard used Jett's version in a commercial that year, Glitter reportedly earned up to $122,000 (č100,000). The computer company only pulled the commercial after receiving multiple complaints, including one from the editor of AbuseWatch.net, Evin Daly. That didn't stop Gwyneth Paltrow and the cast of *Glee* from doing a cover of the song on the show in 2011."

In one section of Keven T. McEnaeney's *Hunter S. Thompson: Fear, Loathing and the Birth of Gonzo*, the Lucy vignette from *Fear and Loathing in Las Vegas* is examined. The story "underscores the dangerous sociological epidemic of unstable daydreamers searching for alternative authority figures in the counterculture to guide them out of whatever family impasse or slump they find themselves caught in." What's more "this theme nicely dovetails into his [Thompson's] double mention of Charles Manson... who had a group of such disoriented young girls in his fateful entourage."

McEnaeney points out that the story is where Thompson jumps the shark from journalism to delve into fiction. He also points out how Carlos Zeta Acosta, Thompson's lawyer companion, was very upset about the Lucy vignette as it made him look bad. Was it simply a tall tale? And if it was, would it be an isolated incident or was there some truth to the tale of taking an innocent young girl, plying her with drugs, and having your way with her?

One of the most widely cited philosophers of all time, Michel Foucault felt that the Marquis de Sade, from whose name the term "sadism" is derived "had not gone far enough," since, unaccountably, he continued to see the body as "strongly organic." Foucault came to enjoy imagining "suicide festivals" or "orgies" in which sex and death would mingle in the ultimate anonymous encounter. Those planning suicide, he mused, could look "for partners without names, for occasions to die liberated from every identity."

James Miller in *On the Passion of Michel Foucault* claims that Foucault's penchant for sadomasochistic sex was itself an indication of admirable ethical adventurousness.

Thomas O'Carroll, is another academic and proud pedophile. O'Carroll has been incarcerated for conspiring to corrupt public morals in 1981 and again in 2006 for making and distributing child pornography. This charge stemmed from involvement with his International Paedophile Child Emancipation Group (IPCE) and its subsidiary Gentlemen with an Interesting Name.

Justin Lee writes in "The Pedophile Apologist" of the conundrum of using "the scholarship of sexual abusers" and the issue of academic work being put "in the service of deviancy:"

"O'Carroll has authored two books, *Paedophilia: The Radical Case* (1980) and *Michael Jackson's Dangerous Liaisons* (2010), the contents of which are easy enough to surmise.

His new article, 'Childhood "Innocence" is Not Ideal: Virtue Ethics and Child-Adult Sex,' will appear in the December 2018 issue of *Sexuality & Culture*, an interdisciplinary journal that 'publishes peer-reviewed theoretical articles based on logical argumentation... and empirical articles describing the results of experiments and surveys on the ethical, cultural, psychological, social, or political implications of sexual behavior.' Ostensibly a serious academic journal, *Sexuality & Culture* does publish the occasional eye-gougingly bizarre piece of 'scholarship,' like the recently retracted 'Going in Through the Back Door: Challenging Straight Male Homohysteria, Transhysteria, and Transphobia Through Receptive Penetrative Sex Toy Use.' O'Carroll's paean to the 'virtues' of child-rape, however, is in a league of its own.

"At 73 years old, O'Carroll has long been a bogeyman for both the left and the right — not to mention the children he has violated. To the right, he's the perfect condensed symbol for the Sexual Revolution's true telos — the nihilistic destructuring of human relations. To the left, he's an albatross, a useful idiot for conservatives intent on establishing a link between homosexuality and pedophilia. He's also a testament to the degraded standards of interdisciplinary scholarship.

"According to O'Carroll in his *Sexuality & Culture* article 'virtue ethics fails to provide a convincing justification for rejecting sex between adults and children.'

" 'The assertion that children are incapable of reciprocal sexual relations is empirically unfounded. Where is the evidence? A comparison with animals is again suggested. Dogs appear to be perfectly capable of reciprocity in loving relationships with human beings, often to the extent of being every bit as devoted and loyal in their affections towards their owners as their owners are towards them, and perhaps even more so. Again, even the personhood-restricting Scruton has acknowledged this (Scruton 2013, 2014). Dogs may lack a sophisticated appreciation of the other's "intentionality", on which Scruton sets so much store as a qualifying criterion of moral agency within sexual relations, but this appears to be no barrier to reciprocity in what many would consider to be its morally essential features. There should be mutual affection and attention to the other's wishes. What else is needed, really? It may be thought this analogy is insufficiently close because dogs are not sexual partners of their human masters. But they can be. Dogs are not shy about expressing sexual interest in humans, and when their owner reciprocates that interest a sexual (and loving) relationship may develop, as has been attested in *Dearest Pet*, a book by Dutch controversialist (and children's writer!) Midas Dekkers, and endorsed in a review by philosopher Peter Singer."

Speaking of the slippery slope, it seems pedophile apologia is not too far distanced from the defense of bestiality in the minds of some academics:

"If even a dog can experience the requisite feelings in a reciprocal relationship of interpersonal (in all but name) character, why would a child be incapable of doing so?"

A longer book than this one could be focused on merely the intellectuals, artists, and authors who have openly supported pedophilia. Just one example recently in the news is Gabriel Matzneff. A central figure in the world of haute couture in France who hobnobbed with some incredibly powerful and influential people such as fashion designer Yves St. Laurent and former President François Mitterrand, who once described Matzneff as a "mix of Dorian Gray and Dracula."

Gabriel Matzneff came to symbolize the French aristocratic/elite double standard as far as pedophilia goes. Matzneff was a known pedophile for decades, writing about it, speaking about it on television. Despite having been reported for sexual abuse charges decades ago, he was never investigated. In fact, all the while he was receiving pay from the Ministry of Culture:

"To sleep with a child, it's a holy experience, a baptismal event, a sacred adventure," Matzneff wrote in his 1974 book "Les Moins de Seize Ans" ("The Under Sixteens"). He wrote about his sex tourism in the Philippines in 1985's "Un Galop d'Enfer" ("A Hellish Gallop"): "Sometimes, I'll have as many as four boys, from eight to 14 years old, in my bed at the same time."

Mehana Mouhou, a lawyer involved in a civil suit against Metzneff indicts the French justice system which she says "has prostrated itself before a writer. Matzneff never hid what he did. He recounted the relations he had with young children whose lives have been shattered and scarred. Ministers, people in the world of culture, politics, the media, let it go and and now we have to ask why they let it go and seek accomplices. Matzneff is just the tip of an iceberg."

Part of Matzneff's legal defense was that it was different times. He also points out how at the time other noted intellectuals such as Foucalt, Jean-Paul Sartre and Simone de Beauvoir and top papers like *Libération* and *Le Monde* regularly defended the idea of sex with children.

"There were all these arguments [in the '70s and '80s] that the child was a person in their own right, that they were fully formed at age 6 and that the family was a prison from which the child had to be liberated. These people argued that sexual relations with an adult were a form of emancipation, and that parents who complained that their child had been abused were only interested in getting money in damages," Pierre Verdrager, French sociologist and pedophilia expert said.

Verdrager also pointed out that there was even a movement aimed at lowering age of consent and eventually getting rid of age of consent entirely. Greek mythology, historical tradition and culture were cited.

Matzneff sailed by taking advantage of "l'exception culturelle française."

To anyone who doubts the normalization effect of the French "cultural exception" to pedophilia, considering the following story from *The Atlantic:*

"On April 24, 2017, a 28-year-old-man met an 11-year-old girl in a park in Montmagny, just north of Paris, after which, he took her home where he had oral and vaginal sex with her. When it was over, the girl called her mother and described what had happened, and her mother called the police. 'She thought ... that she didn't have the right to protest, that it wouldn't make any difference,' the mother told *Mediapart*, a French investigative site which first reported on the allegations of the case. The accusations were of an adult raping a child—a crime that, in France, can lead to a 20-year prison sentence for the perpetrator when the victim is 15 or younger.

But it initially wasn't charged that way. When the case first went to court in September, the man faced only charges of 'sexual infraction,' a crime punishable with a maximum of five years in jail and a

75,000 fine. Under French law, a charge of rape requires 'violence, coercion, threat, or surprise,' even if the victims are as young as the girl in the Montmagny case. When the case, initially postponed, went back to court in February, the man's attorneys did not deny the sexual encounter but argued that the girl had been capable of consenting. 'She was 11 years and 10 months old, so nearly 12 years old,' defense lawyer Marc Goudarzian said. Sandrine Parise-Heideiger, his fellow defense lawyer, added: 'We are not dealing with a sexual predator on a poor little faultless goose.'"

This situation shows the extent of the petitions and activism by Sartre, Simone DeBeauvoir and other existentialists, postmodernists and deconstructionists against the French age of consent laws. In a 1979 edition of *Liberation*, another petition was offered in support of a man on trial for having sex with girls between the age of six and 12. Of the 63 undersigned, many were influential intellectuals. The argument was that the girls were "happy" to take part.

"The love of children is the love of their bodies. Desire and sexual games have their place in the relationship between children and adults." As a result, according to *Liberation* the prepubescent girls' "fulfillment [was] proved to everyone, including their parents, the happiness they found with him."

The idea was that children needed to be "liberated" from sexual mores and "unfair" laws against sex with children. The influence of the "pedocriminal lobby" in France has had long standing effect. The previously mentioned case does not exist in a vacuum, *Atlantic* also cites a 30-year-old man who was acquitted of raping an 11-year-old girl due to the prosecution failing to prove that the sexual act was not consensual.

France of course is where Roman Polanski fled after his child sex crimes were revealed. The child erotica photographer David Hamilton also lived in France, a haven for his type apparently. You can actually purchase two of his films which feature extensive scenes of eroticized, nude underage girls at WalMart.com. Wal-Mart's description of *A Summer at St. Tropez* is as follows:

"David Hamilton creates a new standard in erotic film photography with a lyrical tribute to the grace and beauty of very young women. Hamilton conceives a quiet world in the South of France, where a group of beauties abide together in a remote country house. Their hours are passed unselfconsciously with one another - theirs is an idyllic life of innocence and the intimacy of shared moments is lovingly captured by Hamilton's soft frames. Hamilton has been called a 'master of erotic photography,' for books such as *Dreams of a Young Girl, Sisters,* and his *Private Collection*."

The product description for *Bilitis*, also available at Wal-Mart, is equally frank in it's erotic treatment of barely pubescent young girls:

"A schoolgirl spends the summer with a couple whose marriage is on the brink. Only, the schoolgirl falls in love with the wife. Meanwhile, she pursues a local teenage boy and tries to find a suitable male lover for the wife, so that they can both enjoy an affair simultaneously. Can the schoolgirl accomplish this before the end of summer? Famed female photographer David Hamilton directed this beautifully sensual study of the awakening sexuality of a young schoolgirl, written by a young Catherine Breillat *Fat Girl, Romance, the Last Mistress,* based on the French classic Les Chansons de Bilitis. Unavailable in the US for nearly three decades, *Bilitis* is vintage, French erotic cinema at it's finest."

Hamilton lived in France most of his life enjoying the "cultural exception" we spoke of earlier. It will likely not surprise many readers of this book that he was accused of multiple child rapes before his eventual suicide. One of his victims who came forward, Flavie Flament, lamented the 82-year-old's suicide because, as in the case of Epstein's death, "justice won't be able to do its work."

However, if you so desire, for under $30 you can order his films from Wal-Mart, one of the largest brick and mortar retailers in America. Now if you want a hardcover of Hamilton's erotic studies of 10 to 15-year-old girls you'll have to go to Amazon.com where several of his books as well as films are sold. Jock Sturges, Sally Mann and other erotic photographers who specialize in prepubescent and barely pubescent children mentioned by "PARIAH" are also available for sale at Amazon.

David Hamilton was allegedly only one of a group of "celebrity pedophiles" that, with the permission of playwright Dorothy Hewett, molested her daughters.

Nabokov's book *Lolita* brought a story of forbidden love between a young girl and her stepfather to the masses. In the book *Celebrity, Pedophilia, and Ideology in American Culture* it's pointed out how Humbert seems to suffer from the Victorian habit of accusing the precocious child of being the seductress. Blaming the victim for the actions of the predator.

By the time the 1990s adaptation of the film by Adrian Lyne appeared, the controversy had still not settled. Edward Kofner, editor-in-chief of Media Action Alliance accused *Esquire*'s photo shoot for the movie as "doing its part to desensitize society at large to the real problem of child sexual abuse."

The book later deals with the movies *Happiness* by Todd Solondz and *American Beauty*. Both of whom deal with the father in a family seeking sexual excitement from minors, children in the case of *Happiness*. It's worth noting the fact that Allan Ball, screenwriter of *American Beauty* a story about a middle aged man lusting after a high school girl also was responsible for the movie *Towelhead* which features a fairly graphic scene of sexual assault on a barely pubescent girl.

JON BENET RAMSEY

You can't delve into the connection between pop culture and pedophilia without mentioning Jon Benet Ramsey. The Jon Benet Ramsey story is one of the most haunting media spectacles of the 90s. The O.J. Simpson trial arguably set the stage for reality TV. Even to the extent of being the television debut of the Kardashians. As grisly and disturbing as the details of that story was, it had nothing on the story of a child model viciously sexually abused then brutally murdered.

Jon Benet has an entire section in McGowan's *Programmed to Kill*. That book shone a new light on the whole affair for me. In early 2018 Jeffrey Epstein was still alive, though not nearly as widely covered as he would be soon. I was writing about him as well as other stories that were not getting proper attention like massive grooming and abuse taking place on YouTube, Instagram, SnapChat, Periscope and apps like WhatsApp and Kik. Jon Benet Ramsey's name popped up in the news cycle inspiring me to look back into the case.

A confession had supposedly occurred. I'll admit I ignored it. As it turns out, so did the Boulder, Colorado police department. Gary Oliva, 54, claimed he was responsible for the death of the 6-year-old pageant queen back in December 1996. I picked up the "World Exclusive"

from *Star* magazine in January 2018. And yes, in case you're wondering, I do occasionally read the gossip outlets. Once in a while, the *Enquirer* and their ilk have some real dirt with palpable evidence apart from hearsay gleaned from "sources close to" or other "he said, she said" nonsense.

My guess is Oliva is looking for some fame and perhaps fan letters from women with hybristophilia (a paraphilia wherein one finds themselves attracted to murderers, rapists, and other beyond-transgressive types).

Regardless of the reason for the story popping back up in the news cycle, it had me reaching for my copy of McGowan's *Programmed To Kill: The Politics of Serial Murder*, specifically the chapter on Jon Benet and the farce of an investigation surrounding it.

Jon Benet Ramsey was sexually abused and horrifically beaten. Some investigators believed she looked "re-dressed" after the incident. Not only had rigor mortis already set in by the time she was found in the Ramseys' basement, but authorities reported noticing the strong scent of her decomposing body. Had she survived, she would have been in her 30s today... had she survived.

Dave McGowan wrote extensively about this case in his book. From the start Jon Benet's parents were suspects. John Ramsey was the son of a WWII pilot and, himself, a Naval officer and pilot stationed in the Philippines in the 1960s. His company Access Graphics was bought out by Lockheed-Martin, one of the largest military-defense contractors in the world. Her mother Patsy had also been a beauty queen in her time. McGowan relates how a Miss America judge once referred to her as "a little automaton."

Patsy's father was the vice president of Access Graphics which, even after the Lockheed-Martin buyout, was headed by John. According to Cyril Wecht's book on the case, Patsy's family, the Paugh's, along with John "exerted considerable influence" over Patsy Ramsey.

The night after attending a party with family and friends, John, Patsy, and brother Burke, Jon Benet was put to bed. The next morning, sometime after 5 a.m. Patsy headed downstairs to find a ransom note. It was after this, according to her story, that she checked her daughter's room to find her missing and called 911. At 5:52 a.m. Patsy placed a call to 911. You can hear her plainly saying at first, "Hurry, we need an..." as if to say "ambulance" before catching herself, pausing, and calling for "police."

Three days prior, the Ramsey residence had called 911 on two occasions, the first being on the night of December 23. The Ramseys were throwing a party featuring 100 of Boulder's movers, shakers and high society. The guest list, nor the reason for the call the night of the party has never been shared with the police. One known attendee was Bill McReynolds, who played Santa for the party. On December 26, 1974, the same day Jon Benet was found dead, Bill's daughter had been abducted with a friend who was staying with her for the night. Bill's daughter was released unscathed apart from being made to watch the sexual assault of her friend. No arrests were made, no charges ever filed.

Bill's wife Janet would later write a screenplay, "Hey Rube," about a young girl who was abducted, tortured, and murdered before being discarded in a basement. In 1978, the *New York Times* would refer to the play's subject as that of a "ritual killing," specifically that of Sylvia Likens. The chilling coincidences don't end here though. Bill spoke at the memorial service and mentioned several other children he had known before their similarly unexpected deaths.

According to an interview, McReynolds would carve Jon Benet's name on a harp alongside the names of three other young girls he was close to that had died. For what it's worth, the information regarding McReynolds' harp is hard to find online. The article is no longer available at *Boulder Weekly* online and neither archive sites nor Google cache are much help. Most of the most recent snapshots at Archive.org are also blank, but if you jump back about 15 years, a copy of the original can be retrieved. Equally disturbing, part of McReynolds' final wishes were having the glitter Jon Benet gave him mixed with his ashes.

On the Ramseys' list of suspects, McReynolds loomed high. The kidnappers in their note just happened to ask for exactly $118,000. Luckily for the Ramseys that was the precise amount of John's recently received Christmas bonus pay. The rambling letter purported to be written by the kidnappers mentioned being part of some "small foreign faction" and describes a call they were to receive that morning which was, incidentally, never made.

Allegations that the family intentionally obstructed the investigation by tampering with the crime scene are practically moot when you consider the fact that, for whatever reason, police allowed the crime scene to be breached by the family, friends even the pastor.

Other irregularities also came to light; such as the coroner's late appearance, around twelve hours after the body was found. The coroner spent only ten minutes examining the body. Additionally, why was the couple not initially interrogated separately? Police even charged John Ramsey and his friend, oil company executive Fleet White, with searching the crime scene.

John and Fleet decided the basement might be a good place to check despite White claiming he checked the basement and found nothing out of the ordinary. John Ramsey then picked up his daughter (further spoliation of evidence) and removed the tape from her mouth. McGowan points out that the autopsy reports no tape residue. An officer at the scene was quoted for a piece in *Vanity Fair* noting how John didn't cry coming up, but laying her down "he started to moan while peering around to see who was looking."

Neither of the Ramseys attempted to comfort or console one another during this charade. As for how liable to be true any of the official stories from the Ramseys are, I'll defer again to McGowan:

"The unlikely scenario that we are asked to believe is that an intruder entered an occupied home seeking a victim to abduct, but then inadvertently killed his intended victim, at which time he decided to hide the body in the basement assuming that it wouldn't be found. He then searched the house for pen and paper before composing both an unfinished draft and a final ransom note, the latter of which rambled on at some length."

Dr. Robert Kirschner of the University of Chicago, a child abuse specialist believed it was quite possible that Jon Benet had faced repeat abuse long before all that occurred the night of her murder. "The thing that concerns me is that the hymenal opening is measured at 1 centimeter, which is too large," said Kirschner. "But if in fact, that's the real measurement, that's about twice the diameter it should be. Usually, a hymen in a young child like this should be about 4 millimeters, so without seeing the autopsy photographs, it's hard to say whether it could be an inaccurate measurement, prior injury, or normal anatomic variation."

Despite the fact that the Ramseys were uncooperative and stymied any attempt at a thorough investigation, they would be fully cleared due to DNA evidence that has since been called into question. Governor Bill Owens says he was "stunned" and "appalled" at the Ramseys being cleared. Former colleagues and peers in Colorado agreed that the whole situation was, at the very least "irregular."

It's likely that the truth will never be revealed regarding who raped and murdered Jon Benet Ramsey. It's quite possible that there is no single culprit but with the evidence that is available, it's plain to see that after the crime (or rather series of crimes) was committed, an apparent series of crimes was committed that led to the truth being forever obscured.

Beast Of Belgium: Child Exploitation And Cover-Up In The Marc Dutroux Affair

When rumors of corruption among the highest levels of government began circulating in 2016, the term Pizzagate came to represent the idea of organized child exploitation, torture and murder in America. What many didn't know then and now, is that Pizzagate is far from the only similar story. One of the most harrowing of such tales is that of Marc Dutroux, known as the Beast of Belgium and the cover-up and corruption that led Belgium to the brink of revolution in 1996.

In the wake of the eventual trial, 29 high profile businessmen, local police and members of the state police apparatus, the Gendarmarie, were arrested. 30 witnesses died under mysterious circumstances before being able to testify. DNA tests and hair samples disappeared and other evidence was ignored or destroyed in order to advance the idea that Marc Dutroux, the so-called Beast of Belgium, was the sole monster responsible for the kidnapping, torture, and murder of several girls.

One victim, An's father Paul Marchal, said he doesn't think people will ever forget Dutroux, but fears that people will forget that others were involved in the case. Dutroux's wife, Michelle Martin was an accomplice in Marc's original rash of kidnappings and rapes in the 1980s and also helped with body disposal, driving the van around while Marc was procuring young girls for his basement dungeon and even purchased the cameras and filmed the rapes of the kidnapped girls in the dungeon below Marc's houses. Michelle Martin, by the way, was an elementary school teacher herself.

Dutroux, despite being unemployed, somehow had the money for multiple properties, extensive renovation and construction and was able to rent or purchase elaborate digging equipment that should have been impossible on his government pension for disability. The girls, by the way, were often drugged with sedatives and sleeping pills that the psychiatrist who had ruled he was disabled had prescribed him. In addition, it is quite obvious that many involved in supposedly investigating the growing number of disappearances were obviously involved in some way as they acted to shield Dutroux from prosecution for as long as possible.

Driving around in a white van to kidnap young girls straight off the street then chaining them in literal rape dungeons on his various properties, drugging, raping, and sometimes burying them alive, is horrific in itself. When you consider the implications of how much cover-up was involved, how protected Dutroux was, and the likelihood that he and his wife did not act alone it makes those facts even more bloodcurdling.

Dutroux's first run-ins with the law involved some petty thefts, muggings, and drug dealing as well as stealing cars in 1979. It is supposedly the money he made at this time that allowed him to purchase so many properties and the equipment needed to build the extensive underground network of tunnels and cells on various of his properties.

In 1989 when he was arrested for the rape and kidnapping of five women years earlier, he and his wife were convicted and imprisoned for a time. Dutroux was given a 13 i year sentence. His wife, Michelle Martin, was sentenced to four years. Both were freed far earlier, however. Dutroux himself would only serve three years of his sentence. It was Martin who hatched the plan to escape notice by building underground cells to house the girls in the future. This despite Yvan Stuart's later admission to a parliamentary commission:

"A medical report described him as a perverse psychopath, an explosive mix. He was an evident danger to society."

UK's *Telegraph* reported that Martin's plan was to create a literal underground city in a mine shaft where the girls could be housed. Dutroux claimed he wanted the underground city to actually be a safe place for the girls so they could be protected from the pedophile ring that had him in their service. In 1992, Dutroux was let out over 10 years early "for good behavior." At least five murders we know of and the rape, abduction, and torture of several others took place in the intervening years. It was just three years after his release that Julie Lejeune and Mélissa Russo were kidnapped. The girls were held in a tiny cell in the series of dungeons in one of the seven properties fitted for this purpose. The cells were barely 3 feet wide and hidden by shelves in the wall. The girls were restrained by chains around their necks and barely given enough food and water to keep them alive. The girls were, at other times, unchained so he could violently rape them. Often at these times, Michelle would film the results.

Dutroux told the girls they could write letters home. He would read these letters himself, but obviously, they were never delivered. He also allowed them to keep a diary. One of his 12-year-old victims wrote of each day she was raped. If the rape was painful she signified this with an X. Especially painful rapes were signified with two Xs.

It is shocking to think of how the police easily could have stopped this nightmare before the deaths of Julie and Mélissa, before the kidnapping, rape, and torture of other girls. Julie and Mélissa were only 8-years-old at the time of their abduction. Police received information from four informants who claimed that Marc Dutroux had asked them to accompany him to kidnap young girls to sell them for the purpose of sex trafficking.

June 24, 1995, the first two kidnappings resulted in an appeal from the parents on television. Shortly after that, however, the story seemed to fade away. No longer was it mentioned in the news and the police seemed disinterested in further investigation. The family of the victims hired a local detective who, in turn, hired a criminal profiler. This profiler, Carine Hutsabeut, put together information that should have led to Dutroux being called in for questioning, but of course, that was not the case here.

Shortly after the disappearances of the two 8-year-old children, two teenage girls also went missing. They were last seen alive on stage being hypnotized as they were filmed by someone in the audience. Surveillance video shows them leaving the area for a tram. That was the last family or friends ever saw them alive.

Three weeks after this, in another strange turn of events, a woman writes the police saying she had seen two girls being held who match the description. The woman explains that they are being held by her own son. The woman is the mother of Marc Dutroux. For whatever reasons, despite numerous informants and Marc's own mother saying he should be investigated further in these crimes, police do absolutely nothing. All this time more girls were disappearing that Summer of 1995.

Claude Thirault, one of the informants spoke of how Dutroux had driven him around and pointed out young girls who would "sell well" to a prostitute network he knew of as he suggested kidnapping girls. Thirault went immediately to the Gendarmes to inform them. This was 1992.

Supposedly some distrust and competition between local police and Gendarme is part of the reason why nothing moved forward any sooner. The Gendarme apparently had a confidential file with information related to Marc Dutroux as a suspect.

Once again, it was Claude Thirault who informed the Gendarmes that Dutroux was preparing the underground cells. He was "renovating his basement" he told officials. Once again, if he was not involved in trafficking girls and/or drugs it seems difficult to fathom how he could afford all the equipment, construction and extensive "renovations" and elaborate tunnel systems.

Both local and state police have been informed that Dutroux is likely involved or responsible as they have been asked directly by him to kidnap girls. Why did Dutroux feel so confident? Did he know how protected he obviously was? The guardian of the Gendarmes "confidential file" on Dutroux, Reny Michaud, organized a sort of secret surveillance of Dutroux and his properties. It was known by the codename Operation Othello. Michaud's men watched Dutroux for about five months. During this time the kidnappings did not cease. On December 6 Dutroux was arrested for car theft and placed in custody.

The Gendarmes feared police would search his house. "Don't send a police commissioner, send me, I know Dutroux and have had him under surveillance for some time," Michaud was reported to have implored. They did so. During the search of the house, Michaud and a locksmith found videotaped evidence of the rape of young girls. Also found was a videotape of the parents begging for their children's return. Michaud put "a symbol" of some sort on certain of the tapes which supposedly signified they were of no importance to the investigation. Some of the material on these tapes involved Marc constructing a ventilation system in his underground dungeon, raping a young girl in Czechoslavakia, a group of naked young Romany girls in Romania.

While Michaud and the locksmith made their way into the cellar where Julie and Mélissa were being held they found chains, vaginal cream and a gynecological speculum, Dutroux's prescription sedatives, and sleeping pills. The locksmith testified that he heard children's voices. Michaud shouts, "Silence!" There is no more whispering at this point. The locksmith when questioned by authorities said he begged Michaud not to leave that he had heard children whispering and that they shouldn't leave when there were obviously voices in the cellar. Michaud reportedly replied, "Who is the Gendarmerie official here?"

At this time, Michaud calls off Operation Othello. He reported they had found nothing and that Dutroux was no longer a suspect or person of interest. Dutroux was freed a few months later and at this time is free also of suspicion of culpability in the brutal crimes he played a part in.

In the four months that Dutroux is incarcerated his wife comes to the home to feed the German Shepherds but claims she was too "frightened" to go down to the cellar and feed the girls but that she did drop bags of food. Apparently, the food was just out of reach for the chained girls. In addition, it was Winter in Belgium and no electricity or heat was running. This is one theory of how and why Julie and Mélissa died but to this day the full truth about the case is unknown and the trial itself seemed to create more mystery than closure.

Dutroux takes a heroin addict associate back in the infamous white van, goes scoping young girls to kidnap. They staked out a swimming pool where they find a 14-year-old girl, Leticia. Journalist

Douglas DeConnick reported how at this time the white van had been noticed by multiple people and someone had a part of its number plate. Finally, Dutroux was arrested, along with his wife and Jean-Michel Nihoul for the kidnapping of Leticia. Dutroux, while arrested, confesses also to kidnapping a 12-year-old girl Sabine who had been held captive and raped for 79 days.

One of the victims herself mentions judges and others involved in organized rape. She implicates Nihoul as a sort of ringleader and the connection to the trafficking. Nihoul was said to have a list of children to kidnap and abuse, Jean-Michel "abused children in a very sadistic way" they were taken to sex parties where Dutroux would bring drugs and young girls where those at the upper echelon were allegedly involved. Other girls involved also named influential persons who were supposedly involved in the sex trafficking of the young girls.

Regina Louff has been accused of lying despite her testimony having never changed. It was Nihoul, "the party monster" she says, who invited magistrates, judges, businessmen, and other important personages, "It was big business and it was very well organized too. There's a lot of money going on there and a lot of blackmail too. They had a lot of parties. They filmed it even. So yes, it exists. I know it sounds crazy and there is a big taboo on everything like that, but it exists." The businessman and associate of Dutroux, Nihoul, was cleared of all but drug dealing and freed within five months on that charge.

Dutroux confessed and showed police not only where the living victims were being held, but also where the bodies of four girls, Julie Lejeune, Mélissa Russo, An Marchal, and Eefje Lambrecks had been buried. Julie and Mélissa, he maintained, died accidentally from starvation. An and Eefje were drugged, wrapped in plastic and buried alive.

The investigation into whether a larger network was involved seemed doomed from the start. Officers were taken off the case just as they began uncovering details, witnesses turned up dead. A judge who some family of victims claimed was earnestly working to bring those responsible to justice, was taken off the case. At this time murmurs of conspiracy and cover-up leaked out into the Belgian populace. To this day, several investigators and family members of victims maintain their belief that Dutroux was correct.

The comedy of errors that was the official investigation smacks of a cover-up. The cameras used for Operation Othello were only on during the day time. The tapes, marked with "some symbol" as unimportant were ignored despite them showing the construction of the rape dungeon and rape of girls. Police claimed they were not able to watch them because they did not have a VHS player at their disposal.

Evidently renting a VCR in the '90s in Belgium was far more difficult than elsewhere in Europe and the Western world. On top of the farce of a trial, the number of witnesses who suddenly go missing or are found dead under suspicious circumstances, and Belgium's police chief, justice minister, and interior minister all resigning as the trial begins casts a pall on the official proceedings that followed the negligent, if not criminally incompetent, official investigation.

Investigators were told to cease their work. In one documentary an investigator called off the case has tears in his eyes as he explains "we were coming close to some things, perhaps." Other distressing things followed. Mélissa's parents were refused the right to see their daughter's remains on the grounds it was not good for their psychological state. "What would have been good for us was to be certain."

Eventually, 29 police, prominent businessmen, and Gendarmes were arrested in connection with the suspected pedophile ring. At this time a rash of strikes and demonstrations occurred. The dramatic sight of firemen turning their hoses on official buildings just one scene in the larger drama. Belgium was on the brink of a literal revolution. Meanwhile, radio and television didn't do much to publicize what was going on but still, 300,000 people showed up to march through the streets of Brussels dressed in white with white balloons. The white symbolizing innocence. The innocence lost of numerous young girls involved in the Dutroux affair.

Dutroux was eventually sentenced in 2004. Dutroux maintained till the end he was only following orders from an international pedophile ring he was working with. Dutroux even alleged two policemen were involved in helping him abduct two of the girls. To this day Le Monstre Belge, has left his mark on the nation of Belgium. Over a third of Belgians who carried the surname Dutroux changed it between 1996 and the end of the trial.

Justice Minister Melchior Wathelet, who freed him after deeming Dutroux "fit for society," would be promoted to the hallowed role of judge at the European Court of Justice at the Hague. So if there's any wonder why justice is not seen in these cases of institutional pedophilia, collusion, complicity, and involvement in these crimes by journalists, the rich, the powerful, politicians, police, lawyers, judges, and even royalty should be a hint.

Sadly, this story resembles other cases of organized exploitation of children involving powerful people that have occurred in Italy, Portugal, Lithuania, England and elsewhere.

7th FLOOR GROUP COVER-UP

When the Pizzagate conspiracy was making the rounds much less was written about the 7th Floor group cover up and Operation Flicker On Wednesdays, the so-called "7th Floor group" allegedly would meet and work out which FOIA requests should be squelched. They also edited the Congressional record to delete information that would expose them and their allies. In many cases, we can likely never know what all was hidden.

The Washington Examiner divulged how a February 2013 report by the Inspector General of the State Department was suppressed to avoid embarrassing Hillary just days before she left Obama's Cabinet. The report on the public record was compared to an earlier draft leaked by whistleblower Richard Higbie.

Examiner pointed out "the unexplained gaps" and "removal of passages" between the original, leaked version and the later revised version. Material that could damage the State Department or Hillary Clinton were removed. This "call[ed] into question the independence of Harold Geisel, who was State's temporary inspector general throughout Clinton's four years at the head of the department."

Another censored section of the 2013 report:

"Inspectors learned in conversations with Department employees... that in some cases superiors in [diplomatic security] and in senior levels of the State Department have prejudiced the commencement, course, and outcome of [special investigations division] investigations. [...] Sources referred to [diplomatic security] sometimes circling the wagons to protect favored [diplomatic security] rising stars from criminal charges or from embarrassing revelations that could harm a promising career.

"One case, which triggered outraged comment from several [special investigations division] sources, relates to allegations that a Regional Security Officer engaged in serious criminal conduct including sexual abuse of local embassy staff during a series of embassy postings. Sources also reported that a senior [diplomatic security] official successfully protected some agents on the Secretary's Detail from investigations into misbehavior while on official trips."

Hints of this story first came out in June of 2013. Aurelia Fedenisn, a former investigator for the inspector general of the State Department. Fedenisn spoke to CBS just before the report's release regarding the edits. At that time, the State Department spokeswoman offered a bald-faced lie to attempt to salvage the integrity of the Department. Jen Psaki was confident claiming "the notion that we would not vigorously pursue criminal conduct is preposterous."

It would be years before the original unedited draft would leak making prostitution, drug use, sexual assault, pedophilia, and other charges public.

Fedenisn hired a Dallas-area law firm to represent her against the State Department after she was reportedly subjected to intimidation due to her whistleblower status.

That law firm was broken into just weeks after the CBS report was published. The pair of thieves took only computers and files that contained information about Fedenisn, leaving untouched valuable items that included silver bars, according to the local news affiliate.

Higbie said many whistleblowers like himself fear nothing will change if they take the risk to report wrongdoing.

"If a whistleblower reports a significant amount of criminal conduct that includes viable supporting evidence, some kind of action must be taken that is public," he said. "Otherwise, as is the case with the State Department, current and former employees do not believe coming forward with information that is vital to Congress in its oversight of the Department will materialize into any form of accountability."

A 7th Floor Department official even killed an investigation into an ambassador accused of pedophilia. At the same time, another senior official with diplomatic security stopped the investigation of the ambassador-designate. Bear in mind, in 2010 the Pentagon failed to look into hundreds of cases of child pornography purchases made by employees of the Department of Defense. Sometimes even within the hallowed halls of the Pentagon itself. Some 250 of the 5000 netted in ICE's Project Flicker were civilian and military employees of the DOD. Some with the highest levels of security clearance.

As recently as 2018, it was discovered that DOD's networks were ranked 19th out of nearly 3000 networks in the US for sharing child porn through peer-to-peer networks. *USA Today* in December of 2019 claimed that the US government "lacked the resources" to investigate 80% of those DOD employees.

This story didn't make the shockwaves one might expect, not nearly so much uproar as there was over the Pizzagate phenomenon. The Pizzagate conspiracy went mainstream shortly before the 2016 election thanks to Wikileaks sharing certain leaked emails related to John Podesta, Barack Obama's Chief of Staff and Hillary Rodham Clinton's campaign manager. It all started with some odd usage of the word pizza. In some cases, (like a "pizza related map," whatever the hell that would be) according to several conspiracists the messages made little or no sense unless you factor in how some of these words are known by the FBI as codewords used by pedophiles and organized child traffickers alike.

The story was instantly dismissed by the media but consider the Epstein story's cover-up for years aided by the various reporters and outlets. A *Forbes* journalist accepted $600 to publish an article under his byline written by a PR company Epstein hired. Then there's the case of ABC killing a story about Virginia Giuffre's experience being trafficked by Epstein and the cover-ups by the 7th floor group of ambassadors and government employees having sex with children and downloading child pornography sometimes from government offices and military bases.

The Podestas' art collection, featuring images of children being abused and other disturbing themes, similar art inside Comet Ping Pong, disturbing (and now deleted) posts including toddlers taped to tables from the Jimmy Comet/Comet Ping Pong account and the group Heavy Breathing, practically the house band of Comet Ping Pong, who were accustomed to making regular jokes about pedophilia helped fuel the rumors of something sinister. Whether there was more than some severely disturbing and inappropriate inside jokes at a supposedly family friendly pizza place, perhaps we'll never know and I'd rather steer clear of conjecture, so we'll leave the Pizzagate discussion at that.

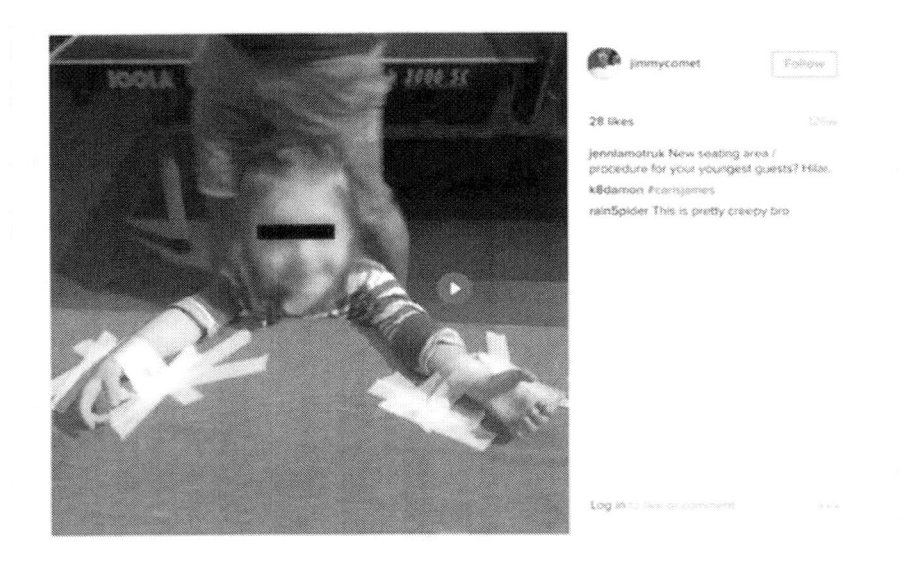

HARRY HAY & THE SAFE SCHOOLS

Safe Schools, eh? But safe for whom? If you mean safe for child predators then I would argue we need less safe schools, as is, the movement towards normalizing pedosexuality has been advancing on school districts for far too long. Many of you may remember the case of Kevin Jennings, for instance. Jennings was appointed the "safe schools czar" over the United States. Jennings was also an advocate of the Gay, Lesbian, Straight, Education Network (GLSEN) pronounced "glisten." In addition to admitting that he once advised a 15-year-old who confided in him regarding a sexual relationship with an adult man to just "use condoms" there are more troubling factors that came to light. Jennings was an unabashed fan of Harry Hay.

Who is Harry Hay? Well, he's one of the primary founders of the North American Man-Boy Love Association (NAMBLA), of course. His failure to discourage a young teen from embarking on sexual exploits with a full grown male maybe makes a little more sense when you factor in his admiration for "radical faerie" and unabashed pederast activist Harry Hay. Here's a great quote from Hay:

"I also would like to say at this point that it seems to me that in the gay community the people who should be running interference for NAMBLA are the parents and friends of gays. Because if the parents and friends of gays are truly friends of gays, they would know from their gay kids that the relationship with an older man is precisely what thirteen-, fourteen-, and fifteen-year-old kids need more than anything else in the world. And they would be welcoming this, and welcoming the opportunity for young gay kids to have the kind of experience that they would need."

Evidently the more... "adventurous" side of gay activism a la Harry Hay didn't disappear from "safe schools" when Jennings left office in the US. Take, for example, the words of Gary Dowsett:

"There used to be a spicy element in gay and lesbian liberation... demands that we can and should fuck anything that moves, as long as it said yes freely. Do we still aim for that? That we can and should fuck anything that moves, so long as it said yes freely. Do we still aim for that? Do we still see the queering of all sexuality as possible? Desirable? Inevitable? The same kind of problem occurs with those other kinds of thorny sexuality issues of the day...

"Why do we need an age of consent at all? Are there diverse kinds of intergenerational sex? And are they always harmful?"

Good Lord, and what does this potentially dangerous pervert do for a living besides trying to "spice up" gay and lesbian liberation by bringing young kids into the picture? Well, that's the really scary part, he's part of the Australian government's "safe schools" program. Ah, but this must be some recent development at least, right? Sadly no.

As far back as 2016, he was being called a "pedophilia advocate" by MP George Christiansen, according to headlines in the *Daily Mail*. This doesn't stem from just a few years ago. Kevin Jennings started working on the radical philosophies he injected into his "safe schools" initiative as far back as the '90s but Professor Gary Dowsett may have him beat by at least a decade.

The Australian "Safe Schools" program was launched in 2010 while Dowsett was Acting Director but his "activism" dates much further back. In the journal Gay Information, issue 11, published by Sydney's Gay Information Service, Dowsett was responsible for an article entitled "Boiled Lolllies And Bandaids: Gay Men and Kids." The article has some prize bits of wisdom like the following:

"First, we have three legal/social questions to win: custody rights for gay men and lesbians; the legal right of paedophiles and their young loves; and finally, the sexual rights of children as a whole.

"And I also have a friend, a paedophile, who is working very hard on making sense out of his relations with boys. Those relations consist of, among other things, a large amount of nurture and support for these boys, a real caring for their welfare and growth.

"How different then is that gentle, tentative sexuality between parent and child from the love of a paedophile and his/her lover? From all their accounts and from many academic studies (some worse than others), that kind of love, warmth, support and nurture is an important part of the paedophilic relationship.

"The current paedophilia debate then is crucial to the political processes of the gay movement: paedophiles need our support, and we need to construct the child/adult sex issue on our terms."

That's right, they aren't child molesters or predators, they're human rights activists. And in fact, a parent who doesn't want one of these folks to have sex with their children is actually not only a bigot, but "abusing" their own children by not allowing them to exercise their sexuality.

To be fair though, let's see what LGBT webzine *Queerty* has to say. They expressed anger in 2009 at Kevin Jennings supporting "mostly awesome gay activist Harry Hay" because he "once advocated for including NAMBLA in gay pride parades." Oh is that all? So maybe it's not that bad, maybe Hay wasn't even sure exactly what NAMBLA was and was just arguing for greater inclusivity in the LGBT rights movement, right?

Well, if you go to NAMBLA.org you can find an article by admitted "child-lover" David Thorstad entitled "Harry Hay on Man/Boy Love." It seems that the pederast community is rather upset with the mainstream LGBT movement for attempting to erase Hay's importance to the pedophilia front.

"Harry was a vocal and courageous supporter of NAMBLA and intergenerational sexual relationships, though since his death many of the assimilationists in the gay and lesbian movement, including its most prominent organizations, have already sought to erase that part of his radicalism (not to mention his Communist roots and vocal critiques of their own accommodationist approach to the powers that be)."

In two now-deleted links available as a snapshot in web archives NAMBLA continues to celebrate Hay and shares the Thorstad panegyric as well as speeches he gave at NAMBLA forums and conferences in the 1980s and 1990s. One such link features comments from a speeches that "were given at a public forum on February 22, 1983, at New York University cosponsored by the NYU gay group and the Stop the Witchhunt Committee, which had been formed to counteract a massive campaign by the FBI and the New York City police to smear NAMBLA as having kidnapped and murdered six-year-old Etan Patz. The episode is documented in the book, *A Witchhunt Foiled: The FBI vs. NAMBLA*, for which Harry wrote a promotional blurb. Other speakers on the panel were John Burnside, Katherine Davenport, representing the Stop the Witchhunt Committee, and Michael J. Lavery, longtime New York gay activist."

Yes, you read that right NYU hosted Hay so that he could speak on behalf of pedophile "rights activists." At this NYU speech, Hay speaks fondly of his youth:

"The point is that I was perfectly capable of handling myself and knowing exactly what I wanted. But this year I knew that I wanted to find a man to tell me what I wanted to know. So, at fourteen, you realize, I'm a child molester. I'm a child, and I'm molesting an adult till I find out what I want to know. And I found him, and he was shocked. Then he discovered that, rather than being a man, as he suspected that I was from the way I looked— my callouses on my hands, and the way I handled myself, and my clothing —that I was only a fourteen-year-old kid, and if anybody found out about it he'd be in jail for life, or, at least in California twenty-three years in that period."

Hay is quite adamant about the idea that pedophilia is not only safe but downright necessary. "Because if the parents and friends of gays are truly friends of gays, they would know from their gay kids that the relationship with an older man is precisely what thirteen-, fourteen-, and fifteen-year-old kids need more than anything else in the world." More than anything else in the world. Those are just a few choice sections from one of his speeches on behalf of NAMBLA though. I will spare you more examples of the same.

So it seems a bit dishonest to claim that Hay "once advocated" to allow NAMBLA to march as *Queerty* claims in their article,"Smear

Campaigns: Kevin Jennings Supported a Gay Activist Who Once Supported NAMBLA. So He's a Pedophile?"

Daily Beast also argues on behalf of Jennings in "Hannity's Gay Target." If the beast is to be believed, pointing out how disturbing having pedophiles in charge of schools equate to an attack on homosexuality. In my opinion, considering that the vast majority of homosexuals aren't pedophiles I would count this as a far greater aspersion: "As Obama readies a major gay-rights speech, the right is tarring his safe schools czar with a homophobic slur. Michelle Goldberg on why the White House must stand by its man."

Clinton surrogate David Brock, and the former lover of Comet Ping Pong's James Alefantis heads Media Matters. Of course, they got in on the fun "debunking smears" related to Jennings. According to them all "right wing attacks" against Jennings were "thinly veiled homophobic appeals." As to the promotion of "child porn in the classroom" Media Matters explains that away as well:

"The organization, however, specifically stated on its book list website that 'some titles for adolescent readers contain mature themes' and recommended that 'adults selecting books for youth review content for suitability.'"

But NAMBLA was but one group Hay was involved in. To continue playing the devil's advocate, let's say that Jennings admires Hay's numerous work and activism unrelated to NAMBLA. Jennings was the president of Gay, Lesbian, Straight Education Network (GLSEN). GLSEN at the very least didn't vet their speakers at the TeachOut conference which introduced children as young as 12 to graphic conversations about sex. In one instance even advocating the practice of "fisting" which led to the Fistgate scandal that made Jennings the ire of conservative talk radio and Fox News.

"Fisting [forcing one's entire hand into another person's rectum or vagina] often gets a bad rap....[It's] an experience of letting somebody into your body that you want to be that close and intimate with...[and] to put you into an exploratory mode." Bear in mind, this event was sponsored by the Massachusetts school system. A parent and member of the group MassResistance was criticized for violating student's privacy when he leaked the videotape of the event.

The actual name of the scandal, however, comes from the erroneous claim that "fisting kits" were distributed. As it turns out, the "fisting kits" were some bizarre "make your own dental dam" kit given to the schoolchildren and, Jennings wasn't directly involved. I certainly wouldn't go so far as to say former US Safe Schools Czar Jennings is a likely pedophile, as Gary Dowsett is, but it seems the idea of introducing children to graphic sexual material isn't much of a concern to him.

This seems to be a trend here though, doesn't it? Let's move to Canada briefly so we can discuss architect of Safe Schools and former Deputy Education Minister Benjamin Levin. In Canada, the Safe Schools program is also known as the Inclusive Education Strategy. One can hope that at least Jennings is the one out of three mentioned here whose idea of "inclusivity" doesn't refer to including pedophiles in positions of power in school administration.

According to the Canadian Broadcasting Corporation, in 2015 Levin "was handed a sentence of six months for possession of child porn, 12 months for making child porn and 18 months for counseling to commit sexual assault." Levin slid by with such a minor sentence due to the fact the judge felt he appeared "genuinely remorseful" and had a low risk of offending as per his psychiatric assessment.

All this despite the fact that Levin admitted online to abusing each of his daughters. In October of 2017, the *Toronto Sun* reported that as of that writing Levin had "been on parole for some time." After spending just over a year in jail, he was first granted day parole to a community-based residential facility in August of 2016. By January he was granted full parole.

Toronto Sun also reports how Levin was finally caught after spending time in chat rooms dedicated to child sexual exploitation and incest:

"In one case, Levin sent photographs to a New Zealand police officer, one showing a 'close-up of the face of a crying child, her face smeared with black makeup.' Levin suggested to her the image was "hot," according to parole board documents. Another photo he sent showed a young female bound and leashed, with a gag in her mouth and Levin commented, 'Mmm, so hot to imagine a mother doing that to her girl to please her lover.'"

INSTITUTIONAL PEDOPHILIA AND GROOMING EPIDEMIC IN THE UNITED KINGDOM

After the Savile scandal broke and hundreds of sexual abuse allegations finally surfaced at the death of the well-known television presenter and so-called philanthropist, Operation Yewtree was launched. Yewtree looked back into accusations against numerous entertainers for the BBC going back decades. The operation resulted in 2,000 suspects but only 19 arrests and of those arrests only six convictions. In the media, it was decried as a witch hunt. Witch hunt or not, the majority of those named by alleged victims remained free.

In the video on YouTube, "Nudge and Wink Jokes about Jimmy Savile (1978-2007)" 40 years of Jimmy Savile pedo inside jokes are showcased making it clear that this was, after all, an open secret within the BBC.

"He loves her slot" presenters joke of an 8-year-old girl who wrote in about the "Jimmy Savile comment slot." In a couple cases you can even see live where after making a joke the hosts or presenters seem to blanche and realize that they may not have a job the next day.

Johnny Lydon, better known as Johnny Rotten, appeared on Piers Morgan Live in 2015. He spoke of his censored appearance on the Peel Sessions where he mentioned wanting to kill Jimmy Savile, "we all know that but we're not allowed to talk about it. I know some rumors." The host warns him it could be libelous. "Nothing I've said is libelous."

Lydon was banned at the "height of the Sex Pistols" despite formerly having badmouthed the royal family. Apparently, singing "God save the Queen, she ain't no human being" was fine, but accusing Savile, or rather calling a spade a spade, was a bridge too far.

"We all knew what that cigar muncher was up to. Not only him, a whole bunch of them." BBC never aired it and he was banned "for quite a while" for his "contentious behavior."

Operation Hydrant and Operation Fairbank (no relation) were also set up to look into 262 separate investigations involving at least 670 institutions where widespread abuse of children occurred and was often covered up.

Not all victims who came forward talked to police and Peter Spindler retired Metropolitan Police commander, felt Operation Yewtree was set up too late to be effective in netting any of the accused high profile pedophiles. 30 detectives looked into "Savile plus others" but, similar to the high profile names connected to Epstein, very little legal action commenced. What little court drama there was rarely resulted in justice for victims.

600 alleged victims came forward between October 2012 and 2015. 450 were related to Savile. Many of the alleged victims had never spoken to the authorities. "The reasons cited for this were varied and included the fear of not being believed and a lack of trust in statutory agencies or feeling that the justice system would be ineffective in prosecuting the offender."

Elm Guest House was at the center of another institutional abuse inquiry but even those who led the abuse inquiry into Jimmy Savile and the others named admitted that the police "got some things wrong." Some detectives working on the inquiry "didn't have the knowledge and skills" needed, for one. To this day, despite the wealth of testimony historical sexual abuse investigations in the UK, as in the US are often belittled as no more than "media witch hunts."

We do know, thanks to ITV's Exposure program from October 2012, that Savile "was hiding in plain sight and using his celebrity status and fundraising activity to gain uncontrolled access to vulnerable people across six decades." As well as that the "vast majority of his victims did not feel they could speak out." Not surprising as the few who spoke out during Savile's lifetime were dismissed by the authorities and sometimes even parents or caretakers.

Savile was interviewed in 2000 by Louis Theroux who broached the topic of "the rumors." Savile claimed he actually hates children. Ah, well good to know. No one who hates children would ever want to hurt them, would they? And someone who hates children would want to host a children's television show and make frequent visits to children in hospitals and schools, wouldn't they?

In 2008 a newspaper that alleged he was connected to child abuse occurring at a Jersey children's home was subject to court proceedings for their claims. This despite the fact that the victims primarily were unknown to each other and could not have coordinated their stories. That "taken together their accounts paint a compelling picture of widespread sexual abuse by one offender."

The key here is that the paper referred to them as victims rather than complainants and was presenting their testimony as evidence rather than "unproven allegations." It was however easy to pin all the scandals on Savile when he died, just like after Epstein, by appearances, committed suicide. Once the scapegoat was gone the story could die with it. Chris Morris' program Brass Eye was canceled after a satire parodying a news report into high profile pedophiles in the late 1990s. This followed the UK Pedophile Information Exchange/PIExchange scandal that members of parliament were involved in.

Savile, of course, was good friends with Epstein's great friend Prince Andrew Windsor. When the Savile case broke it was shown that the BBC itself was complicit in the cover-up of the rape of hundreds of children, male and female. Since then there has been some movement towards attempting an inquiry into historical institutional abuse. Unlike in the US where many scoff at the idea of powerful men and women involved in organized child trafficking and exploitation, the UK is at least paying lip service with their Independent Inquiry into Child Sexual Abuse (IICSA).

The IICSA was set up to examine allegations of institutional pedophilia perpetrated by local authorities, religious organizations, armed forces, public and private institutions as well as politicians and celebrities. After Jimmy Savile died in 2011, hundreds of people came forward to explain how they'd been abused by the DJ and children's television show host. The BBC, several schools, children's home, and NHS sites were found to be sites of abuse. As a result, the IICSA was announced in July of 2014. The IICSA has run into some issues since the beginning from internal controversies to claims of a witch hunt being conducted.

One recent case in the news is related to "fixated paedophile" and disgraced headmaster of the Sherborne Preparatory School, Robin Lindsay. The Dorset County Council has refused to comment on a 25-year-old report that showed that pupils had already brought their concerns to administration five years before Lindsay was finally removed from his position. Survivors of his abuse came forward to Somerset Live and ITV. The reports themselves show that the headmaster had tried to convince at least one student the abuse had only existed in a dream.

Freedom of Information requests resulted in documents related to an inspection carried out by social services in 1993. Lindsay was accused of sexual assault and encouraging the children to "share his bed and joining them naked in the showers." Police had already investigated him in 1986, but the allegations were dismissed as having been made with malicious intent. During the second investigation, Lindsay admitted some of the charges but claimed that the event was open to misinterpretation.

Dorset Social Services let him off with a warning in 1993 but when they were brought back in 1997 the follow-up report was described as "damning in the extreme." It was not until 1998 that the Department of Education finally barred him from teaching. At this time he retired from the school saying he wanted to work on clearing his name. The tribunal described him as a "fixated paedophile" who posed a "serious risk to children" but parents of his pupils were among those who tried to defend him.

One wrote in to a paper claiming that "his only fault is to have a little of the eccentricity that we British are famed for." Lindsay never faced any charges for his wrong-doing before he died in July 2016. The second report from 1997, by the way, is now said to be "lost or destroyed" according to the tight-lipped Dorset County Council. The council claims they will cooperate with the inquiry into how he was allowed to get away with abusing children for so long but are declining to answer questions regarding what happened to the "damning" second report and why he was allowed to continue as headmaster afterward.

Somerset Live reached out to the Dorset County Council with several questions they were not interested in answering, but did offer this statement:

"We are not able to comment any further on the matter. However, if an inquiry is called we would fully co-operate if asked to take part."

Sadly, only 6 percent of crimes related to the Modern Slavery Act of 2015 have led to charges in the UK. Of the 5,145 suspected sex slaves, 2,118 (around 41%) were under the age of 18. There has been a 66% increase in the number of children and teens exploited since last year.

Police have been accused of failing to investigate many of these cases. West Midlands police recorded 295 offenses that only led to two charges. Many of the children are lured from overseas with promises of vacations, modeling contracts and most of them end up being used as child prostitutes in London brothels.

The findings are especially unfortunate for Theresa May who had supposedly made handling sex trafficking in Britain a priority for the first time. The Modern Slavery Act resulted in a new post in the government of anti-slavery commissioner who had the authority to seize traffickers' assets to compensate victims.

In at least a few cases however, (Rotherham comes to mind) authorities were found to be involved in the whole situation. In some cases, the Councillors and police knew that the grooming was taking place but were told not to discuss it because it might disrupt police inquiries. In other cases, "councillors and police" were found to be having sex with the child victims themselves.

Some 19,000 children have been identified as part of the grooming crisis... in 2019 alone. Rotherham, Rochdale, Luton and several other cities are infested with grooming crimes. 1500 in Rotherham

2012. That's out of a population of around 56,000 between 0-17.

Sammy Woodhouse, a Rotherham victim who helped expose the scandal, said she is still receiving reports of current abuse in parts of the country.

"You hear this bulls*** line, 'lessons have been learned', but they haven't learned anything," she told *The Independent*.

"I still hear a lot about the authorities aren't doing things as they should. It's not very often I hear something good and for all different reasons – if the police won't act on reports, people feel they're not being listened to or supported properly, or information not being shared."

In January of 2020, *Telegraph* reported that "an excoriating 150-page report revealed that Greater Manchester Police (GMP) knew of grooming gangs sexually exploiting almost a hundred girls, some as young as 12, 'in plain sight.'"

In one case an 11-year-old in Oxford's buttock was branded with the initial of her British-Pakistani "owner".

Two main factors in this are authorities fear of being perceived as racist... and collusion among those very same authorities, whether they be police, lawyers, social workers or what have you:

"After a five-year investigation, the Independent Office for Police Conduct has just upheld a complaint against a senior Rotherham officer who admitted that his force ignored the sexual abuse of girls by grooming gangs 'for decades' because it was afraid of increasing 'racial tensions.'

The copper, who was unable to be identified, told a missing child's distraught father that grooming was 'P----s----ing', and admitted that 'what with it being Asians, we can't afford for this to be coming out', because the town 'would erupt.'"

Speaking of authorities and caretakers as victimizers, the case of an Ealing Abbey and Benedictine school comes to mind. At this Catholic school a "sadistic and predatory" atmosphere prevailed and decades of cover-ups ensued. Since 2003 alone, four staff members have been convicted of multiple sexual offenses against at least 20 children.

The IICSA pointed out, however, "The total scale of abuse can never be known, but it is likely to be much greater."

The case in Ealing at a parochial school involved sadistic violence and sexual abuse of students. According to the 100 page report: "The atmosphere was sadistic and predatory and we heard that for many children coming to school was terrible. There was a culture of excessive corporal punishment.

"Physical abuse in many cases was used as a platform for sexual gratification and a means by which to instigate sexual abuse. Corporal punishment was also used to punish boys who sought to protect themselves and others from sexual abuse."

Father Laurence Soper, was jailed for 18 years in 2017 on 19 charges of rape and other sexual offenses. He was convicted after skipping bail and spending five years as a fugitive in Kosovo. Kosovo, by the way, is where military contractor DynCorp has been accused of complicity in the abuse and trafficking of both children and adults as well as organs.

THE JEFFREY EPSTEIN AFFAIR

No discussion of organized pedophilia would be complete without at least a cursory survey of the Jeffrey Epstein trafficking crimes. Jeffrey Epstein, a shadowy billionaire whose riches and rise to power are still shrouded in mystery was in and out of the news for the bulk of the last two decades. Only in the last couple years, however, did the mainstream media finally decide it was worth seriously delving into.

Epstein was at the center of a cadre of some of the most powerful people from the world of politics, arts, science, literature, Hollywood and the music industry among other groups. We know that Epstein worked initially by luring Eastern European girls with a promise of a better life. A familiar story we see with some of the "child modeling" groups that act as fronts for child exploitation.

In addition to that, Epstein tended to use the girls he recruited to recruit more girls. Not unlike Keith Raniere of the NXIVM sex cult, the operation resembled a twisted multi-level marketing scheme. Another motif seen with NXIVM that appears in the Epstein case are the use of "women's empowerment groups" that are actually working to entrap girls and young women into sexual slavery at the behest of Epstein and his partner in crime Ghislaine Maxwell.

Maxwell, by the way, was the daughter of suspected spy Robert Maxwell. Maxwell was tied up in the PROMIS software scandal and may have been targeted by multiple intelligence agencies. This is but one reason why to this day there are several who question whether his alleged death was drowning, suicide or simply a disappearance to save his own skin.

Maxwell was also a media mogul. One of his own editors, Roy Greenslade, had this to say after his apparent death, falling nude off of his multi-million dollar yacht:

"He was a man who could not face the ignominy of jail, of being shown to be a liar and a thief. And he very much knew that was coming."

Maxwell and Epstein wined and dined the likes of Tesla's Elon Musk, Google's Sergey Brin, Microsoft's Bill Gates collected frequent flyer miles on the Lolita Express. Eileen Guggenheim was another potent culture-maker who was quite close to Epstein and Maxwell. Guggenheim referred to them as "important benefactors of the Academy" and even pressured a young artist, Maria Farmer, to become tied into the twisted couple.

Victoria Secrets' Les Wexner is also closely tied to the Epstein affair and also was connected to similar art patronage. How innocent this patronage was we may never know but there are numerous examples of the world of high art being used as a smokescreen for hiding assets, cheating taxes, laundering money and committing other crimes.

Before we go any further, a hypothetical: what's the difference between a journalist at a world renowned publication and a courtesan? The high price call girl will have a higher hourly rate.

As John W. DeCamp mentioned, with the aid of law enforcement, politics and the media any size cover up is possible. The situation of *Vanity Fair's* Graydon Carter is an excellent exemplum. He was but one of many who shut down the story before Epstein was arrested, opening the floodgates. Like Harvey Weinstein, Epstein used bribes, connections and threats to keep his dirty deeds in the dark.

Mirroring a scene from The Godfather, *NPR* reported a severed cat head in the front yard of *Vanity Fair's* editor's home as well as a generous donation made to a *New York Times* reporter's favorite non-profit and other veiled threats and inveiglements seemed to keep the media in check. Certainly a factor in the fact that until the axe fell there was "no substantive coverage" of Epstein in the press at large.

David Boies, an attorney for victim Virginia Giuffre has said, "We count on the press to uncover problems, not merely to report on when problems have been prosecuted and when people have been indicted, but to uncover problems before they reach that stage. And here you had a terrible problem. A horrific series of abuses."

So much is still murky about the Epstein affair. How and why was he "tipped off" before the first raid in 2005? According to the documentary series *Filthy Rich*, Epstein "had the resources" to do counter-surveillance on those who were on his trail, including the police. How did he get a teaching job without a degree in education and even more baffling, how did a math tutor rise to billionaire status with no visible paper trail to explain such a trajectory?

Epstein lived in the lap of luxury while having girls aged 12 to 15 serve his basest desires. From erotic massages and exotic dancing to drug dealing and procuring other girls for Jeffrey Epstein's growing stable.

Maria Farmer, the artist, introduced to Epstein and Maxwell via Guggenheim, points to cases of Epstein abusing young girls as far back as 1996. Sadly, her own younger sister Annie included. Maria went to the FBI and was summarily threatened by the sex deranged, quasi-mafioso couple. Reporters were called reminding them there was nothing to look into, in some cases as mentioned elsewhere in the book either investigations were shut down or puff pieces written specifically by Epstein's own crisis PR agency appeared in their place.

Of course when things got too deep and an investigation began, Alex Acosta, Trump's former Secretary of Labor shut the case down and offered an unprecedented "backroom sweetheart deal" that not only talked down Epstein's trafficking but also offered immunity to all named *and unnamed co-conspirators.*

Epstein spent a short time on paper in jail. In reality, he was out during the day "on work release." Apparently during this whole time he was still abusing young girls on a daily basis.

If not for dogged investigative work by the *Miami Herald* it's possibly that Jeffrey Epstein would never have been charged with trafficking and could be abusing girls to this day with impunity.

Some people are allergic to the very word "conspiracy," but conspiracies happen daily and many are far from theory.

"The conspiracy between the government and Epstein was really 'let's figure out a way to make the whole thing go away as quietly as possible,'" Bradley Edwards, a former state prosecutor who represented some of Epstein's victims, told the *Miami Herald* in 2018. "In never consulting with the victims, and keeping it secret, it showed that someone with money can buy his way out of anything."

There is of course more. Lolita Island, or "Orgy Island" as it was also called, technically referred to as Little St. Jef's, seems to have some odd, occult symbology. What appears to be a Babylonian temple can be seen on the island. As for what the many rich and powerful people did on this island with Epstein and his harem of little girls we may never know, but theories of a widescale blackmail operation coordinated by one or more intelligence agencies seems plausible. Epstein and Maxwell certainly had powerful forces in their pocket and money they couldn't account for. Blackmail would be one explanation for both of these unexplained situations.

Immediately after Epstein's death, the theories that he had been killed began to make the rounds. Even amongst "normies" not prone to conspiracy theory the story didn't sit right. The guards were asleep, but inmates could hear him yelling. Shortly before the guards fell asleep computer records in the jail show they were doing some online shopping. It's also coincidental that the cameras happened to be out and the one video of what occurred somehow ended up "lost." Mind you, this is the same jail that held El Chapo after he had tunneled through a cell in Mexico.

Then of course there's the fact that Epstein was supposedly already on suicide watch. Then there's the fractured hyoid bone which suggests possibility of strangling. Then again, as seen with journalist Gary Webb who died of two gun shots to the head, rare and unlikely suicidal feats aren't all too uncommon on this side of things.

If Nick Bryant is right, it's likely Epstein is but one member of an international underage sex ring. It's even possible that Epstein is just the most well known "broker" and was thus chosen as a scapegoat. Regardless the story exposed a dark underworld that implicated some of society's most powerful and influential people. As a result, it's no wonder so much about this case is so foggy.

As mentioned time and again in the book, many of the people at the top of the food chain seem to know about the dirt that goes on behind the scenes, but apparently turn a blind eye in order to remain in the room. Reddit CEO Ellen Pao tweeted the following:

"We knew about her supplying underage girls for sex, but I guess that was fine with the 'cool' people who managed the tightly controlled guest list."

Wait, so you were at a party with a notorious trafficker, knew about it for years and kept silent? How does this not make you complicit? Then again, how different is this from ABC news sitting on the story? Is not their silence consent allowing Epstein to continue? It's a sad but true tale that became especially highlighted after the Harvey Weinstein affair, but sometimes high profile stories disappear when they deal with high profile people. And money does seem to make the world go round.

As far as the matter of money games, Epstein seemed to have been tied up in more than one type of dirty deeds. Epstein went head to head with Scott Rothstein who was charged for running a $1.2 billion Ponzi scheme. In fact, in 2012, he tried to claim that Florida attorneyes were manufacturing the sex slave claims to tip the scales in the Rothstein Ponzi trial.

So what do we know about Jeffrey Epstein? We know that he is a convicted sex offender with a propensity for underage girls. We know that he has powerful friends. We know that great lengths had been gone to in order to keep the court documents free from public scrutiny. We also know that the presiding judge was one Donald Hafele.

But who is Donald Hafele? Well, he is the man who pushed back Epstein's trial in November for one in the following order:

"Under the circumstances of this unusual and relatively complex case, the court finds that there are simply too many significant, lengthy motions that are pending and need to be heard prior to December 5, 2017, the date that the trial was originally scheduled to commence."

He is also the man who seemed hellbent on protecting the serial child abuser who had already negotiated a "controversial non-prosecution agreement" (that extends to his "co-conspirators" of course) that allowed him to plead guilty to the charges of soliciting prostitution and procuring a minor for prostitution. The dozens of other young girls Epstein abused will be able to file civil lawsuits against Epstein's estate. Meanwhile, during the stead of his "incarceration" Epstein enjoyed a fairly open door policy.

Hafele was also dead set on making sure Mr. Epstein's name was secured throughout the case. He had said he would not allow any graphic testimony entered into the record, for one, and has also warned attorney Jack Scarola that in addition to limiting evidence that can be used against Epstein that, "I don't want this to turn into whether Jeffrey Epstein is a serial child molester."

Heaven forbid we call a spade a spade. Meanwhile, where had Mr. Epstein been all this time? According to the *Palm Beach Post* at that time, he spent "most of his time on his private island in the U.S. Virgin Islands." Convenient considering most of the abuse of the sex slaves occurred on his private jets (Lolita Express) and his island (Lolita Island).

If you do the least amount of digging into Hafele you'll see that many Floridians were more than a little perturbed when he was, for whatever reason, appointed to the 15th Circuit court. Now-defunct site Topix.com (local gossip central online) featured multiple users who had their say:

"Charlie Crist receives a name from a local attorney, who was appointed by Crist to find judges for the 15th circuit. This attorney who is located on Palm Beach Lakes, is not honorable in anyway. He is more dishonest and in some hallways of the courthouse, called an Anti-Christ. This attorney who appoints friends of his to the court system, lives in Flamingo Park. This attorney has problems with the local church nearby his home, because he does not like black people and the noise they make during service. But this attorney is working for Charlie Crist on finding judges for the 15th circuit. This attorney is one dumb Gator, but his day will come and he will be will known to everyone of what he and his law firm is really like. Of all the dishonest attorneys out there, this one tops the list of going straight to Hell once he has his last breath on this earth. As for not liking black people, this attorney will have to get use to Obama.

"It is obvious that several posters here are in judge awful's pocket. I have personally observed the 'judge's' biased acceptance of testimony from those whom he had business relationships. The reasoned arguements and testimony of an honest and hardworking citizen was ignored over that of an incarcerated inmate. BTW the 'judge' allowed an uneducated process server whom he knew to act as counsel for the defendant.

This appointment ensures that I will never spend any significant amount of money or time in the state of Florida ever again. I have had first-hand experience with Donald, and found him to be an abusive, unethical, ego-maniac. Check with the Florida bar, and you'll find the same. Thank you Charlie Crist for revealing your poor judgement, and making my decision to buy a house in California that much easier!"

Meanwhile, there's the scandal reported in the *Sun Sentinel* in 2005 before he was honored with the bench seat for the 15th US Circuit court.

The judge tapped to preside over the inquest into the shooting death of a black Delray Beach teen by a white police officer "removed himself from the case on Wednesday amid questions about his ties to attorneys involved in the hearing."

It's also interesting to note the connection between Judge Donald Hafele and Charlie Crist. Crist was connected to the billion dollar Ponzi schemer David Rothstein who said the key to his success was "wooing" politicians like Governor Crist and Senator John McCain. Rothstein says he used his bankroll to "curry favor with politicians, lawyers, bank presidents and cops to create the aura of respectability" necessary to enact his confidence scheme.

He describes a "quid pro quo" relationship with Crist that involves the Governor doing favors for him. Rothstein says one of the "favors" Crist returned was consulting with the Governor in regards to his official duties with the Judicial Nominating Commission.

After Crist appointed him, he said he would regularly consult the governor on which of the applicants should get the nod. When the search committee selected finalists, Rothstein said he made sure those Crist wanted were on the list.

Further, he said, he talked to Crist about who the governor should appoint to vacancies on the Broward County bench. He urged Crist to appoint those he believed would make favorable rulings for his law firm once they donned their judicial robes.

So, in other words, we know that many of Crist's appointees were appointed not for their integrity, but rather for their lack of ethics and willingness to be bought off. Suddenly Hafele's willingness to look the other way in defending a monster makes so much more sense.

Jeffrey Epstein, like so many billionaires and oligarchs, was known initially not for his deviancy but his philanthrophy. Reputation laundering through charity is not only a way to improve one's image but can also open doors. Epstein was a donor to the powerful Council on Foreign Relations (CFR), multiple universities, several scientists (including many working in genetics), Tribeca Film festival and several pet charities of his associate Les Wexner. During Epstein's life he availed quite a bit of reputation laundering via the non-profit industrial complex, many of his donations even being hidden due to tax deductible status.

It's been over a year now since Jeffrey Epstein's death. Sadly, for the moment, no one has seen justice for the numerous crimes against hundreds of innocent, young girls. Ghislaine Maxwell is, for now, being held awaiting trial though there are attempts to have her freed for the moment on a technicality due to the fact that vegan meals are unavailable as an option while she's in lockup.

Thankfully, some materials that had been sealed for years related to a case Virginia Giuffre nee Roberts brought forward have finally been made available but I'm still not holding my breath waiting for any of the big names in the black book or the flight manifest getting so much as a slap on the wrist.

A DIGITAL PLAYGROUND FOR PEDOPHILES

I stumbled across the online group Exposing Exploitation (now Academy Awareness) a few years ago while researching a story about the predators operating in the open at YouTube. Beginning with the hashtag #YouTubeWakeUp on, I ended up in a disturbing rabbit hole. The brazenness of these organized gangs of online predators is shocking. The results to the children targeted, devastating, and irreversible. YouTube is but one of many digital playgrounds for would-be groomers and child abusers. And often, the platforms are derelict in their duties to protect children using their services.

For months Periscope was warned of children being taken advantage of by organized pedophile gangs on their platform. Finally, after some pressure from a small group of journalists and Periscope users, they acted on their concerns. Similarly, YouTube was called out for several months for certain creepy, disturbing, and sometimes sexual videos that show up in the restricted mode of YouTube for kids. Elsagate was one of the first of such YouTube scandals to make major news. Many feature Elsa from Frozen (sometimes in various stages of undress or simulating sex with Spiderman), Peppa Pig, and a creepy series called The Finger Family.

Previously there was no human oversight and algorithms were left to find similar content to feed babies, toddlers, and small children watching YouTube on AutoPlay. Unnerving violent scenarios, sexual innuendo, and other disturbing and purposefully inappropriate videos had been slid in between the scenes for unsuspecting children to happen upon. Even now with the new changes, a video must be flagged by a user before it is sent over for "human review." The company also failed to delineate what would constitute inappropriate videos for children.

Technology writer and artist James Bridle shared his opinion, "Someone or something or some combination of people and things is using YouTube to systematically frighten, traumatise, and abuse children, automatically and at scale, and it forces me to question my own beliefs about the internet, at every level."

Elsagate, however, may just be the tip of the iceberg. Comedian Daniel Tosh exposed a very popular, very dark YouTube channel with videos netting hundreds of millions of views each. The channel, and many like it, features young girls in bathing suits or leotards and often in suggestive or provocative poses and situations. Some theories attempt to connect the possibly CIA affiliated child trafficking cult, The Finders to the videos. At least a few odd YouTube channels featuring users with the names of Finders cult members exist with some seriously odd videos.

As mentioned, though there are only a few people making videos or writing about this, there are a number of people from around the world who, upon becoming aware of this, have tried to rouse YouTube into action and flagged videos. Perhaps YouTube feels muting predatory comment sections and turning their head is worth the enormous ad revenue generated by billions of views and millions of hours of watch time at their site.

In the French and German #YouTubeWakeUp videos, the existence of a tenuously connected apparently international "network" of pedophiles and online child groomers who share videos and tips for finding such videos on various forums online is discussed. Several "child model" agencies that attracted disgusting comments exist to this day, despite the #YoutubeWakeUp controversy making the story I had been covering for years front-page news at *New York Times* and other major venues.

YouTube, *NYT* finally proclaimed, was a "digital playground" and "an open gate for pedophiles."

Most of the exploitative commenters whether in livestreams or in the comment section begin with compliments which become more

PEDOGATE PRIMER

and more sexualized. This is common in situations of child grooming. This type of "real-time grooming" occurs on YouTube and other networks like Periscope (Twitter's live streaming platform). Journalists like Geoff Golberg have spent years trying to warn YouTube and Twitter with very little success. Each time another horror story unfolds it's the same apology and promise to do better. Meanwhile, we're told that Alex Jones and "fake news" are dangerous enough to delete entirely.

Good news: Twitter has removed "First Scope" channel from Periscope

Bad news: Delayed removal has damaged lives of many children. Emailed Periscope suggesting removal on April 27th. Several others, including @RonWaxman, have urged Periscope to do the same for months pic.twitter.com/uJNY7lt51Y

— Geoff Golberg (@geoffgolberg) November 9, 2017

Periscope is far worse. Rampant pedophile networks grooming children pic.twitter.com/9ISPOXT2hu

— Geoff Golberg (@geoffgolberg) November 1, 2017

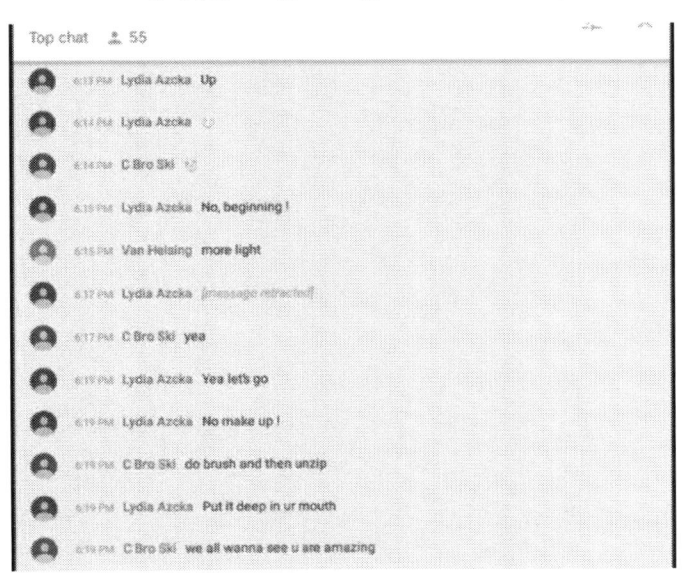

Despite the dire nature of the situation, change is coming slow when it comes at all. Geoff Golberg spent months investigating the

153

massive amounts of grooming and attempting to warn parent company Twitter of the situation.

Forbes, New York Times and other outlets eventually covered the issue briefly, Kik still shows up again and again in press releases from the Department of Justice's Project Safe Childhood.

Videos featuring gymnastics, dance, exercise, performing normal routines, (sometimes including bathing, showering or dressing for bed) are generally the most infested. As the German and French videos mention, many of the most popular videos are from children in Latin America and Eastern Europe or Russia. Then there are the "PedoDare" videos which involve strangers flocking to sites like YouTube and Periscope and mobbing the livestreams with the intent to encourage children to perform in a sexualized manner.

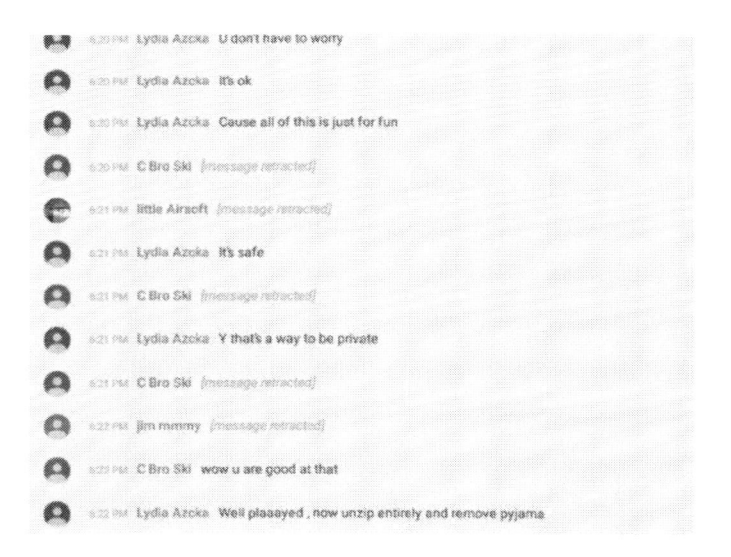

Since this issue has been brought up more and more "predatory comment sections" are being shut down, but some of these videos are still netting millions of views, still likely among hundreds or thousands of others being circulated and reuploaded in pedophile networks. Blocking the offender from commenting also doesn't necessarily block these same abusive, predatory commenters from finding ways to contact the children in the videos either.

"Trusted Flaggers" who spoke to BBC and *The Times* say they feel like their hands were tied and YouTube wasn't doing enough to help. BBC's Trending found that complaints regarding videos related to child exploitation were terribly backlogged.

And it makes sense if you look at it from a purely fiscal standpoint.

When *Buzzfeed, BBC, The Times,* and other well-known media sources had brought their complaints up multiple times it eventually culminated in several major advertisers pulling out.

It was after this that YouTube finally dropped Greg Chism's Toy Freaks channel, a channel in which Chism would have his two young daughters dress up as infants engaging in bizarre behavior such as spitting on each other, "wetting themselves," regurgitating and screaming in fear.

Afterwards, YouTube released a written statement: "We've terminated the Toy Freaks channel for violation of our policies. We will be conducting a broader review of associated content in conjunction with expert trusted flaggers." Many other offending channels featured videos of children confined in small spaces, tied up and "frequently include gross-out themes like injections, eating feces, or needles." Many of these videos had view counts in the tens of millions.

Could one reason behind the reticence of YouTube to act be related to the immense amount of ad revenue YouTube is raking in from pedophile-friendly content? Toy Freaks was one of the top 100 accounts in all of YouTube. Same with Seven Super Girls (one of the SevenAwesomeKids network of channels). When Tosh did his story on the SevenAwesomeKids network he pointed out their over 12 billion views to date.

Buzzfeed spoke to some former stars of the SevenAwesomeKids channels:

"Then some of us started to get the feeling we were being groomed for some darker audience," a former SevenAwesomeKids performer said. "Things that didn't feel weird at the time — like the themes, the leotards, and the camera angles — started to feel strange.

I started to get that feeling especially when you think that some of these girls are 9 years old."

Rylett had a bit of a reputation of being somewhat creepy among the kids and some of the parents, but as he was doling out monthly checks of up to $20,000 each, few complaints rolled in. The girls themselves, by the way, were forbidden by Rylett to contact each other directly. Afraid of them comparing notes possibly? He was described as being manipulative and wielding control over the talent as well as their parents. This seems self-evident in the fact that, for whatever reason, some parents decided it would be a good idea to drop off their child ("under sixteen" is all we have to go on from the arresting documents regarding age) to his Orange County hotel room.

Rylett supposedly had created a "parents committee" to keep the talent safe, but it's certainly possible the parents he chose were picked for their willingness to do whatever it took for fame or money, rather than in the interest of the children's safety. The girls also had to deal with a mixture of threats and promises:

"He'd talk to our parents and tell them to yell at us; he'd threaten to take our videos down; his language was so hostile and the way he talked about the girls' bodies, clothes, and makeup," she said. "It was scarring — you have to understand, these are 12, 13, 14-year-old girls he's doing this to." Another SevenAwesomeKids vlogger said Rylett often dealt directly with the younger girls himself, outside of the view of parents. "A lot of parents early on didn't understand or know what YouTube really was and they weren't really involved. My parents would've flipped out if I told them how Ian behaved, but I was so in love with YouTube I didn't want to freak them out."

A former associate also spoke with Buzzfeed: "It's another example of how YouTube isn't doing anything for us — I've contacted them and heard nothing back."

Another former SevenAwesomeKids performer who spoke with Buzzfeed said she had already contacted YouTube:

"YouTube's responses were not satisfactory," she said. "I think it was like barely three sentences with no real information."

"In all my years filming for the channels, there was never any conversation with YouTube. There was no kid rep support that I know of and no number to call to report things to," another former SevenAwesomeKids YouTuber said. "We were on our own." Buzzfeed reported that at least one of the SevenAwesomeKids channels was taken down, but mirrors of the content are all over YouTube to this day.

The website *Tubefilter* reported on Rylett's plea deal which resulted in him serving only 90 days instead of the possible 15 years in prison he could have faced on the charge of lewd and lascivious molestation. Rylett was put on "supervised probation" for five years and his contact with all minors except his daughter has luckily been restricted. He is also not allowed to contact the victim or her mother.

YouTube made a statement to *Tubefilter* in response:

"We take safety on YouTube very seriously. We work closely with leading child safety organizations and others in our industry to protect young people. When we're made aware of serious allegations of this nature we take action, which may include terminating channels upon conclusion of an investigation."

Comments related to "wardrobe malfunctions" and other "creepy" and controlling behavior were standard for Rylett.

Then there are the multiple "family channels" on YouTube with parents accused of either psychological and/or physical abuse of their own children making millions. In the case of channels like DaddyOFive or the Toy Freaks the channels were deleted while Ace Family and others remain.

The New Statesman pointed out that YouTube is a "haven for abusers" pointing towards the likes of Austin Jones and other YouTubers who have groomed multiple victims. Then there is the recent case of Shane Dawson and the Ace Family who don't seem to have been hurt by the public outing of their inappropriate behavior regarding small children.

Ironically the *New Statesman* reports on how only other YouTubers seem to be exposing the issue with some of those "exposing" the problematic YouTubers being later alleged or accused to be sexually abusive themselves. Onision called out Shane Dawson who called out Jake Paul for being a bad influence, for instance.

Chris Ingham is another "family youtuber." His victim admitted to feeling "scared" and "unsafe" when Ingham allegedly sent her messages inviting her to go skinny dipping after a period of online grooming. To Catch a Predator's Chris Hansen has also touched on the cases of accused groomer Gregory James Avaroe better known as Onision as well as the emo singer Dahvie Vanity. Many who have worked with Vanity allege he has spent years grooming and bedding very young girls.

"It's YouTube's algorithm that connects these channels," said Jonas Kaiser, one of three researchers at Harvard's Berkman Klein Center for Internet and Society who, according to NYT "stumbled onto the videos while looking into YouTube's impact in Brazil." "That's the scary thing."

After Matt Watson's video, *Wired, New York Times* and other major outlets began to say what people like the Exposing Exploitation crew (now known as Academy Awareness) myself and even comedian Daniel Tosh had been for quite a while.

Many YouTubers were quite upset at Watson. YouTuber MistaGG claimed Matt was just trying to "burn YouTube's pockets" while others said that Youtube's quick fixes "won't stop the pedos" which it apparently didn't. Likely never even slowed them down, rather drove them underground. The Matt Watson controversy was blown up into the claims of a witch hunt and Keemstar on his YouTube gossip channel DramaAlert basically called Watson a fraud and claimed the whole #YouTubeWakeUp movement started with him, which it certainly didn't. He just stumbled upon it after others like Academy Awareness did the legwork.

Mista GG and others claimed the attempt to expose YouTube was merely due to him being "a fucking failed YouTuber." MattsWhatItIs did help bring attention to the media of what was going on and launched him into the spotlight of a global controversy creating Adpocalypse 4.0 along the way.

Other's felt Matt's video's end result was merely to "censor and defame the entire #YouTubeWakeUp community" and "compromise the mission of child protective campaigns." In the end, as with Disney, it seemed that sending a message and saving face was most important to the video sharing site. Despite how Matt Watson's controversy eventually outshined the actual story it was clearly important that the "hidden business practices" of YouTube were, for a moment, partially exposed. Unfortunately, YouTubers made it about Matt Watson and ignored the actual situation of child grooming facilitated and profited off of by YouTube and their advertisers.

Exposing Exploitation/Academy Awareness was not even the first to notice a problem on the site. Videos going back around 2009 or earlier reference the term "PedoTube" or "GroomTube" and the YouTubeWakeUp hashtag was apparently started by a French YouTuber, then a Spanish video was made on the subject. YouTubeWakeUp predated Matt Watson by years.

When called out YouTube responded that the situation was "deeply concerning," once again disabling many videos with children running the accounts. The 30-year-old agency Belankazar "specializing in training, representation and management" of models and "improvement and personal growth of the individual" advertises how they train models and organize fashion events.

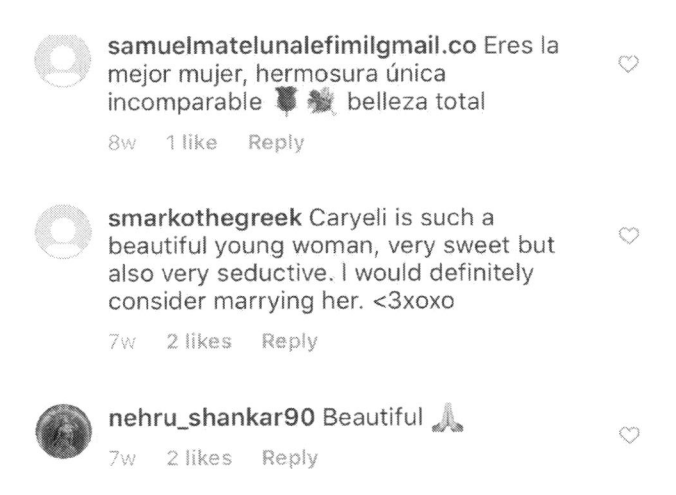

> **samuelmatelunalefimilgmail.co** Eres la mejor mujer, hermosura única incomparable 🌷 🌸 belleza total
> 8w 1 like Reply

> **smarkothegreek** Caryeli is such a beautiful young woman, very sweet but also very seductive. I would definitely consider marrying her. <3xoxo
> 7w 2 likes Reply

> **nehru_shankar90** Beautiful 🙏
> 7w 2 likes Reply

Mainstream news finally covered it after many users pointed out the sexualization of minors and disgusting comments. Comments notwithstanding it seemed Belankazar was obviously catering to pedophiles. Whips and other props that appeal to various fetishes frequently appeared in the runway videos. At least one video was removed related to Belankazar and their membership program which promised discreet payments for extra footage.

"The girls sometimes look for a boyfriend with money who can sponsor them, then when they've drained the poor guy out of all his money they'll dump him and find another. Of course, they are beautiful so it's not hard for them to convince a man to date them," a head at Belankazar told *Daily Mail*.

Sources from within the "beauty factories" of Venezuela spoke of butt implants in some girls by age 12. Of "waists crushed into painful straps for weeks" as well as intestines removed by 16 or painful mesh sewn into the tongue making eating painful.

The head of the Belankazar "beauty factory" said that the average age for a girl to get a breast implant is 16. He said: "To be a beauty queen the breasts can't be too large or too flat. Often the surgery is just to change slightly the shape or the size. It also depends on which contest the girl wants to compete in."

Sometimes it is the girls who choose to do these things, or sometimes it is the parents choice, and sometimes both the girls' and the parents' decision.

Even *Cosmopolitan* picked the story up after the *Daily Mail* talked to Belankazar academy in the article "Good Birthday Gifts For Venezuelan Beauty Queen Hopefuls: Lip Gloss, Silicone Butt Injections." The *Cosmo* piece also emphasized the "long, and scary" surgical procedures list that young girls may face in order to be molded into beauty queens.

The Belankazar academy's owner, Alexander Velasquez, told *The Daily Mail*, "'I don't believe Venezuela has the world's most beautiful women, but we know how to produce beautiful, perfect women. That's why we excel in all the international competitions. And with thousands of girls prepared to put themselves through years of prep at academies (think Barbizon, but more extreme), there are likely to be many poised and perfect beauty queens exported from the country, like a sort of national 'produce' or product, for years to come still."

Twitter user @Bluntsxpusxy shared screenshots regarding the Belankazar memberships.

"Which leads me to my next point. Their model site offers a variety of memberships. The memberships range from from SILVER which include the following: All the PhotoBooks of Minis, Pre-Teens, Teens, Misses and Boys. GOLD which includes everything mentioned above, PLUS -"

@Bluntsxpusxy

Sep 1, 2019

"all special fashion events and photos. And DIAMOND which includes everything mentioned in SILVER and GOLD with an exception that it contains all special Thematic PhotoSessions with their top models and little top models, PLUS access to exclusive Private Special Videos."

@Bluntsxpusxy

Sep 1, 2019

Whether through greed or laziness links like these signify YouTube's complicity in child exploitation. Some of their advertisers now found themselves embroiled in quite a mess. When I covered the convicted rapist and pedophile who ran the SevenAwesomeKids network of channels, I detailed how some models were earning $20,000 per month - envelope-pushing, borderline softcore child pornography is big business at YouTube. Several million users, accounting for billions of views subscribed to the channels in the SSG network.

YouTuber MattsWhatItIs made a list of advertisers whose videos aired amidst questionable material related to young girls. Many of these videos are flanked by a toxic cesspool of a comment section (complete with timestamps of upskirt shots or other compromising sections) ogling risque images of children.

Verge reported in February of 2019 how 2 years earlier YouTube was pressured to update its policies due to the "ElsaGate" scandal which featured strange, creepy often violent, disturbing or sexual content appearing disguised as children's content. YouTube also closed some comment sections on children's videos in order to block pedophiles from posting sexual comments. Before that in 2013,

Google and YouTube attempted to block "exploitative content" from appearing in their search engines. *Verge's* article pointed out that, to date, "YouTube still hasn't found a way to effectively deal with apparent predators on its platform."

To this day there are still disgusting comment sections primarily related to these "child model" or "child star" channels that turn a blind eye to the obvious salivation of pedophiles in their comments section. Many of these channels have a "donate" button since several were demonetized so YouTube still gets to take a cut on the pleasure of pedophiles viewing intentionally sexualized minors.

Youtube's number one concern seems to be profit motive and since their parent company, Google was bought out by Alphabet and dropped "don't be evil" from their guiding principles it seems all options are on the table to achieve said profit.

As much as YouTube seems to be a hunting ground for pedophiles, the top spots for children to be approached, groomed or exploited are still currently Zuckerberg platforms. Namely Facebook, WhatsApp and Instagram.

Facebook also was rightly criticized for a bizarre survey asking how to handle private messages in which an adult asks a 14-year-old girl for explicit photos. Reporting the crime to the police oddly enough was not one of the options. From "this content should not be allowed on Facebook, and no one should be able to see it" to "this content should be allowed on Facebook, and I would not mind seeing it."

The survey went on to ask what should be done about this material, once again, reporting to the police was not an option. Choices given were: "Facebook users decide the rules by voting and tell Facebook" and "Facebook decides the rules on its own."

I mentioned predatory "child model agencies" earlier. One specific example among many follows.

For nearly as long as the internet has existed pedophiles have used it to network, share child pornography, and discuss topics related to targeting children. In recent years, however, social media and apps have become a stalking ground for predators. Roy David

Evans Jr., was sentenced to 17 years in federal prison for sexual exploitation of a child to produce child pornography and related charges after he used Craigslist and the messaging app Kik to entice and coerce a 14-year-old victim to produce sexually explicit videos.

Evans had initially posted an advertisement on Craigslist claiming to be in search of "young models." He directed them to contact him through email or Kik. Kik is a popular messaging app that supports text messages as well as sending images, videos or live cam recordings. A few years back, Kik was referred to as a "dark corner of internet messaging" by *Forbes* for what they referred to as its "huge child exploitation problem."

Back in 2016, Thomas Paul Keeler II was arrested. Keeler was a registered sex offender and huge fan of Kik for all the wrong reasons. Keeler was a member of over 200 Kik groups such as "kidsnbabies" which were used by pedophiles to trade child abuse images. Some of the victims in Keeler's stash were as young as three and "engaged in sexual acts with adults" according to the warrant. Keeler shared materials with up to 300 different individuals in under a year according to the authorities.

As of the *Forbes* articles' writing over half of the 15 million monthly active users were in the 13-24 age range. *Forbes* conducted a joint investigation with *Point Report*, posing as 14-year-old girls. In addition to being flooded with pornographic materials and predatory users via decoys, *Forbes* and *Point Report* uncovered how Kik wasn't deleting profiles of users who had been charged and convicted with child abuse related offenses.

Forbes followed up just a month later and found that Kik was still hosting profiles of convicted sex offenders including those with a history of abusing children. Kik had promised to invest $10 million in making the site safer by the time of the writing of the September 2017 article. The *Forbes* decoy found 10 predators in under 2 hours even after the previous promise of tightening down on the platform to ensure the safety of its vulnerable, younger users.

Child safety experts warned of the major flaws in the company whose valuation is over $1 billion.

"They could change things, absolutely. They could build in much more responsive mechanisms in terms of privacy and safety, they could provide warnings," Sonia Livingstone OBE, professor of social psychology in the Department of Media and Communications at the London School of Economics warned.

"It looks to me like Kik hasn't done any kind of risk assessment, they've allowed for anonymous communication without sufficient privacy and safety controls." If the case of Roy David Evans is any sign, then Ted Livingstone, Kik's CEO's commitment to making the platform safer may need to employ new tactics.

Livingstone offered a statement to *Forbes*: "We encourage users to report content that they believe violates the Kik Terms of Service and Community Standards. Users are also able to block other users they no longer wish to chat with or ignore chats from people that they don't know. Actions are taken against users found to have violated Kik's community standards and terms of service, including removal from the Kik platform where circumstances warrant.

"The other is through education and partnerships with organizations that help adults and teens understand the challenges of today's online landscape and how to avoid bad situations. For years, we've had teams dedicated to this, and we will continue to invest in those types of tools, provide resources to parents, and strengthen relationships with law enforcement and safety-focused organizations.

We want all users to be safe on Kik and will continue to make Kik a safe, positive and productive place for our users to interact. We are continuing to increase our investment in this area, as safety is a priority for us."

In a search warrant related to the arrest of another Kik predator, Michael Stanley Clark, the investigator explained the popularity of Kik with a certain segment of its older audience, "Kik Messenger is frequently used by individuals who trade child pornography because it is free, simple to set up, easily accessible, potentially anonymous and allows users to share digital data privately." Apparently, despite promises from the billion-dollar app, this is still very much the case.

Evans initially pled guilty in April. Upon release, Evans will be registered as a sex offender and is sentenced to lifetime supervised release for his charges of sexual exploitation of a minor to produce child pornography, possession of child pornography and receipt of child pornography.

US Attorney Robert K. Hur explained the sentence, "Roy Evans took advantage of anonymous Internet messaging services to encourage minors to send him sexually explicit images of themselves. This lengthy sentence should send a powerful message that sexual exploitation of children to produce child pornography will not be tolerated in Maryland."

"With ever-increasing access to communication platforms, we must continue to stay a step ahead of those who exploit technology to facilitate the worst crimes in modern society," Cardell T. Morant, Acting Special Agent in Charge, HSI Baltimore added. "Today's announcement serves as a significant marker in our fight against these heinous criminals, and I proudly commend the investigators bringing such criminals to justice."

Evans admitted to coercing three minor victims to produce and send him sexually explicit material. He also admitted to sending three of those images and videos to himself via the internet and even traveled to Montgomery County, Maryland in an attempt to have sex with a 14-year-old victim. At least three minors were victimized by Evans according to his plea and evidence presented.

Pedophilia related products are also becoming fair game. One of the most recent, but not the only, example are baby jumpsuits with disgusting slogans like "daddy's little fuck toy," "I only look illegal" and "daddy's little slut" that were finally pulled by Amazon after massive public outcry.

Marci Hamilton of the child advocacy think tank Child USA spoke with *The Sun* newspaper about the items, "It is shocking, and I'm surprised it is there in the first place. It has a way of normalizing the activity [child sex abuse] which is extremely dangerous to children. It is the first time we have seen such wording aimed at pedophiles on clothing for babies. [Amazon] should have much better controls over products for children generally."

And yes, you read that correctly, it was Amazon the world's largest online retailer who facilitated the sale of these products until just recently. Bear in mind that Confederate flags and anti-vaccine documentaries are strictly prohibited from sale at Amazon, but child sex isn't considered as much a taboo on the Internet's largest marketplace.

A company called DVKFP were selling realistic, child sex dolls with guaranteed "hidden delivery." One of the dolls featured a small, undeveloped child with a little girl's headband. In another photo, the doll appeared to be a young teen with torn clothes and a gag in her mouth.

Don't worry though, of course the offensive items have been pulled due to the publicity. Here's a statement from Amazon themselves:

"All Marketplace sellers must follow our selling guidelines and those who don't will be subject to action including potential removal of their account," an Amazon spokesman said in a statement. "The products in question are no longer available."

Oops, that's actually a statement they made years earlier after getting busted profiting off of child sex dolls sold to pedophiles.

To be fair, their most recent statement was nearly identical:

"All Marketplace sellers must follow our selling guidelines and those who do not will be subject to action including potential removal of their account. The product in question is no longer available."

Their go-to answer whenever something they banned and claim not to sell anymore ends up in the media. Between July and August of 2017, several articles were published in the US and UK regarding Amazon selling child sex dolls. UK's National Crime Agency (NCA) has reported that "these purchases can indicate offenses against children."

Just September of 2020, the latest and perhaps most disturbing Amazon sex doll scandal occurred. A Boca Raton mother spoke with local news about a sex doll that had illegally used her 8-year-old daughter's likeness. According to the Amazon ad, the $559 child sex doll was "a high quality sexy dolly live dolls for men." A local NBC affiliate confirmed the story and also found another website that featured the doll nude.

Then there's Caroline Bosmans, who are vying for the Comet Ping Pong award for creepiest Instagram posts involving children. Recurring themes include children posed in sexualized or dehumanizing ways. Other odd scenarios that keep resurfacing are suffocation, children posed as if drugged or dead, and the use of heartwarming catchphrases like "Eat People."

Caroline Bosmans also apparently loves posing kids in medical situations. In one, a child in a hospital bed surrounded by medical equipment features carolinebosmans comment:

"The kid is alright #alwaysfunwiththiskid #bruisednotbroken" this is just one of many "promo photos" of injured or bruised children. In another post, a picture of a little girl bending over, exposing her underwear is accompanied by the hashtag, #Readytoafterparty? A pervert in the comment section replies, "I'd like to join her ;)". The Caroline Bosmans account answers: "But first some cocktails!"

There are multiple examples of Bosmans Instagram pictures with children bending over, often accompanied by inappropriate comments from followers of the children's clothing brand similar to those at the Belankazar YouTube. However, for many people, this sort of behavior is considered far less dangerous to kids than "conspiracy theories." Priorities, once again...

The internet is a veritable playground for predators. According to recent statistics, one in five children are solicited for sex online. WhatsApp, Kik, Snapchat, Periscope, Instagram, Facebook, YouTube, and other sites and apps become the hunting ground for predators in search of young children to groom, blackmail and sometimes even facilitate meetups for sex.

As a result, there have sprung up dozens of groups who seek out pedophiles by posing as children. *New Statesman* reported on the "morally dubious trend" of YouTube videos featuring vigilantes who entrapped pedophiles, exposing and shaming them online.

The New Statesman article makes some good points about the potential violation of entrapment laws and how untrained vigilante groups can hinder legitimate law enforcement investigations.

NBC reported the story of how POPsquad (Preying On Predators) had "lured" an attempted predator by posing as a child. The manner in which they reported on the story, however, raised some concern among many.

The article begins with a glowing description of the would-be abuser:

"Malcolm was tall and handsome. The oldest son of Jamaican immigrants, he wholly subscribed to the idea of the American dream. In high school, Malcolm was vice president of the Future Business Leaders of America club, assistant captain of the tennis and swim teams, and a member of the student council and Model United Nations. He started a social marketing business at 15."

To create sympathy, friends explained that it was "not easy to be black, Jamaican, a Jehovah's Witness and gay in Torrington, Connecticut" add attempted predator to that list and no doubt, it was a tough life for Malcolm.

NBC's Brandy Zadrozny laments how Malcolm, hanged himself becoming a victim of "mob justice vigilante mentality."

She then goes on to speak of "copycats of To Catch A Predator" like Justin Payne, Creep Catchers, and others before introducing us to POPsquad:

Facebook has helped them reach a growing and rabid audience, and tap into a hunger for vengeance. Local and national law enforcement have begged these predator hunters to stop. Prosecutors say their involvement hurts cases. But there are other, more familiar, consequences.

— Brandy Zadrozny (@BrandyZadrozny) January 2, 2019

Zadrozny names the group Truckers Against Predators (TAP). Anthony Greene of TAP was subsequently locked out of his Facebook account due to the article which put pressure on the social media giant. In a statement, Facebook said they want to prevent anyone from "being publicly shamed" and that what these groups are doing amounts to cyberbullying.

Meanwhile, Facebook-owned WhatsApp was mentioned in *TechCrunch*:

"Google & Facebook fed ad dollars to child porn discovery apps." After a *TechCrunch* report earlier in December about the rampant sharing of child pornography and active child exploitation, Google "scrambled to remove third-party apps that led users to child porn sharing groups." With 1.5 billion users and 300 employees moderating, it's no wonder the problem is out of control.

Facebook has since suspended several accounts, posts, and at least one group while, according to NBC, others "voluntarily removed their own pages to escape what they saw as a purge."

According to NBC, Malcolm was the victim in this situation. They talk to friends who bemoan the "awful" comments posted about him in light of his suicide.

POPsquad's Incognito tried to explain his position to Zadrozny. "He is not innocent. He is not a victim. He tried to create a victim."

Lt. Bart Barone of the Torrington Police Department considered the whole thing, "a sad situation" seeing as Malcolm "was a young kid." Not as young, of course, as his attempted prey.

NBC makes sure to mention "unrelated charges" facing some of the pedohunters in their article all the while attempting to create sympathy for the people who trawl the internet for children, engage in sexual conversations, sometimes sending lewd pictures before attempting to meet them for sex.

Ohio director of state investigations for the Internet Crimes Against Children Task Force pointed out, as was mentioned in *New Statesman*, that some of these vigilante groups do, in fact, jeopardize potential prosecution. Incognito, until the NBC story, was anonymous, but the article shared his appearance making sure to mention his tattoos and history of "hustling." When she shared the story, once again she made sure to mention "dozens of vigilantes - some with criminal records."

Zadrozny called out the ensuing "insane moral panic" that she said was "fueled and informed by trolls" related to a story by fellow NBC reporter Ben Collins who shared an "exclusive" story about trolls posing as gay men "to falsely link LGBT acceptance to pedophilia."

"Everyone who fell for this: No one 'supports' pedophelia [sic] This insane moral panic is fueled and informed by trolls.

Take an Internet break." Zadrozny said in a tweet.

Zadrozny also emphasized in one, now deleted, tweet at the time I covered it how Malcolm is "black, Jamaican, a Jehovah's Witness and gay" without once mentioning the rather pertinent detail that he had also planned to meet a child for sex.

This sort of loaded language makes it fairly obvious where she stands on the issue. At the time I was writing about it, with over 240 replies and 21 retweets but only 38 likes, it was obvious that Zadrozny's story had been, to use some Twitterspeak, ratio'd. Incognito, by the way, had been featured once in a segment with Chris Hansen.

The case of Alain Malcolm wouldn't be the first time an attempted predator would decide killing himself was an easier way out than dealing with the consequences of their actions. Chris Hansen's popular Dateline program To Catch A Predator ended shortly after one of the subjects of the show committed suicide.

Nigel Sheratt killed himself after being exposed by the group Soul Survivors. David Barker also committed suicide when he was outed by the UK group TRAP.

In the war on child exploitation, there is no room for errors that would play into the predators' hands, and with press like this, who needs enemies. Vigilantism is obviously a flawed tactic whose risks outweigh any potential benefits in the long run. And violence against abusers or suspected abusers that could allow the men to go free robs victims of their chance at justice. Not all who are working to combat online exploitation of children are working as vigilantes, however.

A single person always carries within them the innate spark of potential that can create a momentous change in the world. A movement, an impassioned and committed team of individuals, will change these dark realities and feel empowered knowing that in whatever small way they assisted and did contribute to the course of justice and providing a safer environment online.

Meanwhile, Mark Zuckerberg owned Instagram was reported to be the biggest social media platform for child grooming online. 32% of recorded cases of child grooming over a 6 month period came from Instagram. Another 23% of instances took place on Zuckerberg's Facebook with another 14% of cases originating at Snapchat. As recently as May of 2020, the National Society for the Prevention of Cruelty to Children (NSPCC) released data culled from Freedom of Information requests that showed that at least a third of online child grooming takes place at Facebook-owned applications including Facebook, Facebook Messenger, Instagram and WhatsApp.

NSPCC also found a sharp uptick in cases from the 6 month period beginning in October 2019 and expect "a sharper increase this year" due to coronavirus lockdowns as well as "industry failure to design basic child protection into platforms."

Just 15 years ago, it was 1 in 7 children solicited for sex online. As of Fall 2019, the number was 1 in 5 children under 12 solicited or groomed online. If we don't do something in another 5, 10 or 15 years, it might be 1 in 3.

EPILOGUE: The Cuties Controversy

I had completed the bulk of this book around the time that the controversy around the movie *Cuties* began making the rounds. As a result, I felt the need to add this epilogue regarding the film and its reception. As far as the mainstream media goes, the prevailing opinion of the pundits and cinema critics is that only right wingers, fundamentalists, and fuddy-duddies could possibly criticize the film. It is actually a touching film that argues against the sexual exploitation of children, they claim. Well, couldn't that have been done in a way that doesn't involve close up shots of the crotches and buttocks of 11-year-old girls in skimpy, skin-tight clothing humping the ground and twerking?

Peter Bradshaw in his *Cuties* review "Netflix's controversial child exploitation film is bold, flawed - and misunderstood" appeared in *The Guardian* September 14.

He mentions several "sequences showing a group of naive, excitable 11-year-old girls in a dance group twerking and pouting their way through a grotesquely sexualised adult routine." Despite this admission, Bradshaw places blame of the film upsetting several people on an "ugly and abusive social media storm, dominated by vicious trolls." The "offending scenes are gruesomely unwatchable -- deliberately so." That said the film presents, according to the reviewer a "lot more good faith than Twitter and its pitchfork mob." A *Decider* headline urges their readers to "Watch 'Cuties' on Netflix For Yourself, Then Apologize to Maïmouna Doucouré." *NPR* claims the film is being "criticized for calling out the hypersexualization of young girls." I think it's more so the intentionally provocative and sexualized closeups of preteens performing moves more suited to a strip club, personally.

Time also makes the argument that the film is being unfairly criticized when in actuality, "'This Film Is Sounding an Alarm'" according to Cuties Director Maïmouna Doucouré. A documentary film exploring how TikTok, Instagram modeling and companies like Belankazar exploit children might have done a better job sounding such an alarm. Even an animated feature for adults or even the film itself without closeups of young girls groins as they twerk and simulate sex acts might be more appropriate. If one wishes to oppose animal cruelty, actually abusing animals on film might not be the most productive way to raise awareness about the situation.

"This film tries to show that our children should have the time to be children, and we as adults should protect their innocence and keep them innocent as long as possible." Well certainly so, but don't the 11-year-old girls who were sexualized for the purposes of the film count as well? After a petition garnered hundreds of thousands of signatures, Netflix apologized for the "inappropriate artwork" but the scene portrayed in the US promotional material is actually tame compared to some of the scenes in the film itself. Once the movie was released more people were horrified by the sexualization of the little girls than the marketing materials, regardless of whether they were presented "without any context" or not. Netflix also changed the film description as well, changing "twerking crew" to "free-spirited dance crew."

A user warning at IMDB regarding the film possibly being "distressing" due to the intensely sexual scenes involving children was removed by the site. *Distractify* seems to admit that the film sexualizes children but argues that it's "nuanced" exploitation:

"*Cuties* is trying to critique the sexualization it depicts, although most of those coming after the movie don't allow for that level of nuance."

Time mentions how the film "received overwhelming support and acclaim from the international film industry, the French government and viewers in France" but then again so did the erotic nude photography of young girls by accused serial child rapist David Hamilton. Again with "l'exception culturelle" mentioned previously in this book.

It seems the director's aim was admirable, but her execution was more than a little flawed. "Stories of young girls who are 12 years old and prostituting themselves. All of these stories just made my blood run cold, and it made me even more determined to make this film, and to speak out about this issue that is so prevalent in today's society," Maïmouna Doucouré explained. Perhaps these chilling interviews could have resulted in a powerful documentary themselves.

There is obviously a positive message of the dangers of a hypersexualized world "where 'likes' have become the currency of self-esteem and keeping kids away from anything on the Internet is near impossible." Two of the most common defenses of *Cuties* are that the film was acclaimed in France and at Sundance. The co-founder of the Sundance film festival, by the way, was sentenced just last year for raping a 7 to 9-year-old girl.

There is almost certainly politicization of the film in its wake as well. Little good can become of the politicization of the very real danger of child abuse and pedophilia, especially when coopted for partisan purposes. I would disagree with *Vulture* and others who claim that the "anti-Cuties cause" can be chalked up primarily to "various trolls and conspiracy nuts."

Writer Claire Heuchan points out how "revealing" it is that the first major Netflix feature to center on young black girls "hinges on explicitly sexualising 11 year old children. Whether it's acting or music, a sexualized image is too often the price of mainstream success for Black women & girls. Disgraceful."

Rolling Stone, New Yorker, and other major publications have chalked up the "obsession with pedophilia" the film has sparked as a purely right-wing moral panic. Being upset at the highly sexualized images of 11-year-old girls on Netflix "could be protecting actual child predators" according to E.J. Dickson at *Rolling Stone.*

In fact, *Rolling Stone,* like many others, seems to connect any activism against pedophilia online into a mixture of moral panic and even anti-Semitism:

"The tactic has an extensive history that traces all the way back to medieval anti-Semitic allegations of blood libel to the Satanic Panic of the 1980s."

Tulsi Gabbard was accused of "going Qanon" when she opposed the

film. *Rolling Stone* goes on to conflate accusations of pedophilia by anyone as having their "roots in conspiracy theorist circles, such as the Qanon community."

Myself personally, I don't check someone's politics before being disgusted at crimes against children. I do agree that the politicization of child exploitation is a problem and this serious issue should not be reduced to a "rhetorical cudgel." That said, being concerned about a film that features highly sexualized scenes that fail all 6 points of the Dost test doesn't necessarily mean you also believe that Hillary Clinton eats babies and the Qanon strawman is all too convenient to handwave away any legitimate concerns.

YouTuber Max Karson uploaded "Cuties: An Uncomfortably Honest Review" shortly after the movie was released at Netflix. At the time of this writing, his video has over 263,000 views with 78,000 downvotes and 1.3k upvotes.

Karson had previously done an Ask Me Anything thread at Reddit:

"To respond to the most common questions--I'm fairly left-leaning politically (you can be a liberal and also provocative), I have never deleted posts for the purpose of hiding my views (they're all over my channel and the internet in general), and the idea that I'm a psychopath, while seductive, is not true. I just say what's on my mind and that freaks people out."

His review of *Cuties* certainly freaked several people out. Perhaps it was a bit too much information for many. He admits that the film is "basically akin to child pornography" and backs up those "sanely saying, it's exploitative." He also admits that even if you're doing a movie about child exploitation you can do it without exploiting children.

After this things go a bit off the rails. His thesis seems to be that the film is "roping you into the discussion of sexualizing children by sexualizing children and by making you complicit in that." It gets far worse though.

"I don't know if you've ever heard of the app TikTok. There's some pretty interesting stuff on there. That I've checked out and I recommend you check out. Girls of all ages (and guys) are dancing like this. Dances have become more explicitly sexual." As we've mentioned there's always a new app whether it's WhatsApp, Kik, Instagram, Snapchat, or TikTok that predators will use to seek out children. I disagree however that criticizing the sexualization and grooming of children through these mediums makes one "sound the same as old fogeys did in the 50s and 60s."

Karson goes on to explain how "it starts to feel surreal when they're wiping their hands on their crotches from the back if memory serves me. I'll have to watch it again and again and again." He talks about how you "see them shaking their booties on the stairway as they make this viral video and they're pretty hot. You can say whatever you want about me it's not my fault I didn't make them do that. They did that."

Classic victim-blaming attitude again. The point regarding the sexualization of these children that upsets so many is that there are people like Max Karson out there watching this. Also, the fact that the children likely don't fully understand the intent of their actions, just doing as they're directed and as the script demands.

"You're supposed to be sitting there holding these two thoughts in your head," Karson explains, "one that these are kids and the other that they're hot."

It seems that Karson's view of the film would be similar to that of several pedophiles, that the film is mainstreaming child exploitation and that that's ok. Karson posits that the viewer is "supposed to be informed that you are capable of that and that you feel that way. I think it's a good thing to put that out there. Artistically, I think that's a good thing." Somehow Karson can believe this is the subtext of the film while admitting that on some level it's just plain wrong.

"Now is it exploitative? Yes, these kids are 11 so they don't really understand what they're doing." He also asks "should parents allow their children to be in films like this? I don't know.

"If you have a daughter who is 11 and likes doing sexy Tik-Tok dances where she's shaking her ass all the time and some well-meaning and I assume not creepy director comes along and says I'd like to pay your daughter to shake her ass, I guess I would say yes."

Regarding a scene where the main character posts a picture of her vagina on Instagram, Karson complains that "we're more ok with an 11-year-old girl doing drugs or stealing or hurting somebody than we are with her taking a picture of her vagina and posting it on the internet which could lead to something harmful, but in and of itself is not really doing anything too bad to anybody."

Karson also feels that a lot of the "overreacting" surrounding the film can be chalked up to religious fundamentalists and right-wingers.

Cuties is, according to Karson a "solid film" and "better than most movies" though "this film does try to make you sexually aroused by 11-year-olds... and I'll say it's not bad at it. It's not a total failure in that regard to me." Though his opinions are rather disgusting it is at least, as promised, uncomfortably honest. He's blunt when he points out that "there are probably thousands of people masturbating to this film as we speak."

It's "not porn" many argue, that said 8kun (formerly 8chan) owner Jim Watkins, former 8chan administrator Joshua Moon and 4chan administrators have forbidden stills because they violate all 6 factors of the Dost test. Imageboard admins pointed out that certain scenes from the film violated Dost standards and would be pulled from the site as child exploitation material due to the emphasis on the genitals.

"The United States vs. Dost created a six-factor guideline as to whether a piece of media constitutes child pornography:

Whether the focal point of the visual depiction is on the child's genitalia or pubic area.

Whether the setting of the visual depiction is sexually suggestive, i.e., in a place or pose generally associated with sexual activity.

Whether the child is depicted in an unnatural pose, or in inappropriate attire, considering the age of the child.

Whether the child is fully or partially clothed, or nude.

Whether the visual depiction suggests sexual coyness or a willingness to engage in sexual activity.

Whether the visual depiction is intended or designed to elicit a sexual response in the viewer."

Not all points even need to be met to be classified as child pornography but some scenes from *Cuties* seem to hit all 6 points right on the nose. Dost notwithstanding, *Slate* also blames the backlash at the film on conservatives and is another major outlet calling the concern "creepy."

UK's *Telegraph* took a different tactic calling *Cuties* "a provocative powder-keg for an age terrified of child sexuality."

The film is certainly provocative and has become something of a powder-keg, but arguing that those who don't defend it are just "terrified of child sexuality" sounds like the same kind of argument Karson was making.

There are several intentionally uncomfortable scenes in the movie. In one scene the young girls are stopped by security guards and to get past them they decide to twerk for them. Smacking their own and each others' buttocks repetitively, grabbing their crotches with their legs splayed and other scenes gratuitously sexualize the young girls involved.

Maybe 5-10 minutes could be cut from the movie to get the intended message across without being exploitative, without sexualizing the preteen girls.

As for the argument that it's just Qanon followers, the far-right and religious fundamentalists who disagree with the tactic the film took, this can be disproved quite easily. The YouTuber Vaush, with 220k subscribers, identifies as a leftist and often criticizes capitalism in his videos and streams. He was quick to point out that the execution of *Cuties* left a lot to be desired.

Vaush explains in his video "Netflix Tries to Capture the Pedophile Demographic, With Mixed Results" that he is a "big proponent of art for art's sake" but had issues with *Cuties* as a coming of age tale. He contrasts it with the anime *FLCL* as far as dealing with a "child discovering their sexual maturity." He admits that the politicization of pedophilia smears are a "really easy dig." Furthermore, he takes offense at how "discussions on the systemic abuse of children in a sexual manner are always managed really, really dishonestly, especially by the right." Later Vaush goes on to say Hollywood is certainly rife with pedophiles, "this isn't like a crazy conspiracy issue."

I would agree that "both sides weaponize accusations of child abuse." For that matter, harboring child predators and corruption are two of the most truly bipartisan issues that exist.

Cuties, however "fuels the fire a bit" with "a bunch of 11-year-old girls in stripper clothes." Like Karson, Vaush admits that there will certainly be many a pedophile not at all interested in the message merely "cranking it to many, many extremely provocative dance scenes." Furthermore, he found it "really weird to frame it as a feminism thing."

Vaush agrees with the core problem of how media and culture seems to "hyperfetishize youth for girls" and infantilization in general in the West. The way advertising and pornography both "associate youth with desirability" and especially how often in pornographic videos girls are always 18, "a ton of porn is like just turned 18, barely legal, hold up your driver's license," featuring fresh out of high school girls. Vaush points out that the jailbait subreddit despite being "safe for work ostensibly" was a huge subreddit featuring mostly bikini pics of underage girls but with several people in DMs trading child porn. Reddit only shut it down when mainstream media attention was brought to it.

In the end, Vaush argues "we need to socially disincentivize the fetishization of youth."

Twitter also features several self-described leftists taking offense at the idea that opposing filmed child exploitation is a right-wing issue.

"Film studies student here. Also a leftist. it's not the audience that sexualizes these kids. The camera work in cuties is, for lack of a better term, disgusting. the way these girls are filmed is literally just the male gaze a la Megan fox in transformers but with kids."

Another Twitter user points out: "No. Leftists aren't defending Cuties. Only some media outlets defend it. NO ONE is defending this."

"I have not met one queer person who supports cuties, the people on leftist twitter DESPISE any form of child sexualization. The 'pronouns in bio' type are the same type of people who would kill someone for liking a 17 year old anime girl.

Idk what makes you think we endorse pedos"

"oh ok, so because QAnon is railing about Cuties I'm supposed to just shrug & support 11yr old girls looking & performing like porn icons & making themselves look available for others' sex appetites. Sorry, fuck off, I'm not that kind of leftist. Never will be, sorry to disappoint"

"I'm a leftist working class 60yr old mother & grandmother & I've always *hated* the sexualization of children whether in southern childrens pageants or a film like Cuties & I've condemned it. I also happen to regularly rail about every day brutal economic conditions faced by the poor working class that my friends, family & town have to deal with. Sorry, but I'm not gonna apologize for opposing turning 11yr old girls into porn icons."

"I actually decided to watch the Cuties film and this comparison is actually exceptionally gross. A lot of the sexualized scenes in Cuties served 0 purpose to the plot, and things just 'seem to happen'. It was overall unnecessary for them to do the things they did in that film.

The whole film was just gross and the whole message of 'being critical of Western culture sexualizing children' didn't really seem to hit that hard and more or less just felt really uncomfortable all the way through."

"hating Cuties isn't a right-wing thing, it's a human decency thing. i'm incredibly leftist and still wanna see Netflix burn over Cuties."

"Alot of leftists and Liberals are not okay with the 'Cuties' movie. It's one thing both Liberals & Conservatives are agreeing upon."

"Do people actually think leftists or 'the left' supports Cuties by netflix? Almost everyone was criticizing it besides a few blue check marks. Why do these losers like to take a few stupid people and try to make propaganda out of it? This is so dumb."

Meanwhile, it's not the majority of leftists, liberals, or progressives defending the movie so much as the primarily corporate-controlled mainstream media.

Meanwhile, several self-identified leftists and liberals at Reddit and Twitter have also been quick to separate themselves from such critics, perhaps contributing to the disparity between the critic score and audience score for the movie at Rotten Tomatoes.

Left-leaning YouTube commentator shoe0nhead has 1.52M subscribers. Her video on Cuties had 1.5 million views at the time of this writing. She was one of many people online who took offense at the claims that only conservatives refused to defend *Cuties*.

"But anyway can we please not give the concept of being against pedophilia to the right-wing... or any wing for that matter. It's really gross how this is very obviously being forced into some political partisan issue."

Later in the video she pointed out that the very idea that only right-wingers opposed the movie originated with certain media fixtures and verified Twitter personalities:

"I see a lot of blue checkmarks and like journos defending this and I don't know if they're being paid or if this is another case of what I've called in the past compulsive contrarianism. Like the right is mad about this therefore we the left need to defend this."

As for Tulsi Gabbard tweeting about it, shoe mentions the *Jezebel* story that announced she was "peddling Qanon-approved conspiracy theories:"

"Child trafficking is not a Qanon conspiracy and *Cuties* is absolutely softcore, if not just straight up, child porn." The cause gets lost in the controversy surrounding the very real exploitation of the young girls in the movie:

"No matter the intention, it's still sexualizing kids and that's bad."

At Reddit one user noted the narrative of "an alternate reality where leftists are defending Cuties."

Another Reddit user cites another controversial French film that features brutal scenes of simulated rape:

"*Irreversible* was done by adult actors and actresses. They could reasonably know what they are getting Into.

Footage from slaughterhouses is footage being taken of something bad already happening.

My issues with *Cuties,* real young girls are doing these things on camera. Can they give consent? Do they truly understand what they are attaching their name/visage/reputation to? This could have easily been animated and removed the need to have children twerk on camera.

I'd be interested to know what education they provided the young girls who auditioned/got the part about these very practices they are speaking out against. Did they know this was a 'male [sic] you uncomfortable and think' film, or were they lured by the promise of being in a movie and fuck the rest?

I'm okay with being uncomfortable from a movie. Just not when young girls are paying the price with their bodies for it."

In the entertainment subreddit another user broke it down:

"The issue is that children can't meaningfully consent to having erotica of them filmed, so bc they film the erotica of children without their consent, it's an inherently immoral movie, because it victimizes those actors. Ironically exploiting children is still exploiting children."

"Thank you I'm a Democrat and this shouldn't be a right vs left issue this is ridiculous that this is being politicized. This should be a let's not sexualize kids thing it's disgusting, like I know what they were going for and they could of done it differently and still made the point."

In a comment on the /r/movies subreddit an op-ed from the director of the movie *Cuties* likens the movie's failure at expressing it's message to Upton Sinclair's *The Jungle*:

"When Upton Sinclair wrote *The Jungle*, he made a similar acknowledgement. The book was supposed to be about the unfair labor practices and worker exploitation of Chicago meat packing factories, and Sinclair's deliberate intention was to make his novel's message an endorsement of socialism and labor reform.

Instead, audiences were disgusted by the written depiction of the slaughtering and processing of cows. This scene only comprised a single chapter of the book, but that chapter alone left the most lasting impression on readers. Instead of carrying the story of the surrounding 80% of the book, *The Jungle*'s legacy instead stands as a literary influence towards more humane treatment of meat animals and improved sanitary practices in these factories.

While the book succeeded in one regard, Sinclair considered the book an ideological failure at the execution level. Bringing it back round to the topic at hand, Sinclair's words ring very true when it comes to movies like *Cuties*.

'I aimed for the public's heart, and by accident I hit it in the stomach.'

The intent of a creator may be well-meaning and they could believe they conveyed that message effectively upon final review of their work. But the intent doesn't mean anything if the public's reception to it differs this dramatically."

The subreddit r/trashy asked people to "please stop posting about Cuties here" because they "don't want or need screenshots and videos of scantily clad children."

"There's this insane meme going around that if you find this movie distasteful you are 'right wing', and right wing stuff gets deleted.

It's nuts. America's hyper-partisanism is becoming so extreme that people are now willing to accept obvious child exploitation in order to get a win over 'the other side.'"

In one post at Reddit, it was pointed out that moderators of controversial imageboard 4chan pointed out that any video or stills from *Cuties* would be banned due to their explicit content. Ironically, a moderator in that post also warned against this. "Linking images or videos of the trailer will result in your comment being removed for violating reddit's global rules regarding sexualizing minors.

Anybody that posts a comment containing a link or image after this sticky post goes up is also getting a warning or a ban, if appropriate."

It's also ironic that this movie has raised such a furor while shows like *Dance Moms* and *Toddlers in Tiaras* are not too far off from the same type of content. Another point brought up by many individuals online is that 11-year-old girls are dancing suggestively, imitating sexualized music videos on apps like Tik Tok.

As we've mentioned previously though, there is far worse out there than *Cuties*. Some of the most blatant examples mentioned in this book would be the photography and films of David Hamilton. There are many more though. Brooke Shields was just 11 when she starred in the movie *Pretty Baby* where she played a child prostitute. It featured nudity of the prepubescent Shields.

Brooke Shields says she has no regrets about doing the film but when asked by *Vanity Fair* if she would allow her child to do the film she was quite clear:

"In this environment and with social media and with the dangers on that level and just being a mom now, looking at my 11-year-old girl, I would not facilitate it."

It wasn't the first time Shields had been photographed nude, however. At the age of 10 photographer, Garry Gross took nude photos of Shields that appeared in the Hugh Hefner-owned magazine *Sugar and Spice*. Shields' mother Teri attempted to sue Gross when Brooke's star began to rise arguing that the photos could cause "irreparable harm." The New York State Supreme Court however dismissed the lawsuit in a 4-3 decision. Justice Edward Greenfield claimed the pictures were "not erotic or pornographic" except to "possibly perverse minds."

Greenfield also pointed out Teri Shields seemed to want to "have it both ways" profiting off of her daughters appearance in *Blue Lagoon* and *Pretty Baby*. As we mentioned previously in the book, from Shirley Temple's "Baby Burlesque" films through *Pretty Baby* and on to *Cuties* the overt sexualization over time is self-evident.

BIBLIOGRAPHY

Pedophilia in the Victorian Era:

1 https://www.telegraph.co.uk/books/authors/jm-barrie-evil-genius-or-a-misunderstood-ingenue/

2 Dudgeon, Piers; Captivated: The Dark Side of Never Never Land

3 Trilby the Novel That Brought Us Svengali, https://longreads.com/2017/02/16/the-novel-that-gave-us-svengali/

4 Harding, James (Gerald duMaurier: The Last Actor Manager (1989)

5 Birkin, Andrew J.M. Barrie & the Lost Boys: The Love Story That Gave Birth to Peter Pan by Andrew

6 https://www.straightdope.com/21343693/was-the-author-of-em-peter-pan-em-a-pedophile

7 Maggie Tonkin Mandy Treagus Madeleine Seys and Sharon Crozier-De Rosa; Changing the Victorian Subject from University of Adelaide Press

8 BBC documentary "Secret Life of Lewis Carroll"

9 Neverland: J. M. Barrie, the Du Mauriers, and the Dark Side of Peter Pan (review) Anita Tarr, Children's Literature Association Quarterly Johns Hopkins University Press, Volume 35, Number 4, Winter 2010

10 Psychoanalysis and Contemporary Thought, 15(2):199-239 Vladimir Nabokov: A Case Study in Pedophilia, Brandon Centerwall

11 Hiding in Plain Sight: Nabokov and Pedophilia Brandon S. Centerwall, M.D. Texas Studies in Literature and Language Vol. 32, No. 3, Artistic Tensions: Tradition, Society, Memory, and Gender (FALL 1990)

12 https://news.artnet.com/art-world/was-lewis-carroll-a-pedophile-his-photographs-suggest-so-237222

13 http://www.prisonsfoundation.org/uploads/6mem-theendofpeter.pdf

14 https://www.smithsonianmag.com/arts-culture/lewis-carrolls-shifting-reputation-9432378/

15 Woolf, Jenny The Mystery of Lewis Carroll

16 Studlar, Gaylyn. "Oh, "Doll Divine": Mary Pickford, Masquerade, and the Pedophilic Gaze." Camera Obscura, vol. 16 no. 3, 2001, p. 196-227. Project MUSE https://muse.jhu.edu/article/7980/summary

17 Historicizing affect, psychoanalyzing history: Pedophilia and the discourse of child sexuality S Angelides - Journal of Homosexuality, 2004) https://www.tandfonline.com/doi/abs/10.1300/J082v46n01_02

18 https://www.wikizero.com/en/Jack_the_Ripper:_The_Final_Solution)

19 https://www.nytimes.com/2016/11/18/opinion/oscar-wilde-a-refugee-of-his-time.html

20 Murray, Douglas; Bosie: A biography of Lord Alfred Douglas

21 https://www.britannica.com/biography/Beau-Brummell-English-dandy

22 https://timalderman.com/2016/01/27/gay-history-the-cleveland-street-scandal/

23 https://www.telegraph.co.uk/finance/property/4811529/Inside-story-19-Cleveland-Street.html

24 DeCamp, John W. Franklin Cover-Up

25 Brandeth, Gyles https://www.stuff.co.nz/world/europe/94069315/were-there-two-jack-the-rippers

26 Wilson, Karina https://litreactor.com/columns/lurid-the-picture-of-dorian-gray Karina Wilson

27 McGowan, Dave Programmed to Kill: the politics of serial murder

28 http://www.qxmagazine.com/2011/05/nightmare-on-cleveland-street/

29 Simpson, Colin; Chester, Lewis & Leitch, David "The Cleveland Street Affair"

30 Hyde, H. Montgomery The Cleveland Street Scandal

31 Edmonds, Antony Oscar Wilde's Scandalous Summer: The 1894 Worthing Holiday and the Aftermath

32 McGowan, Dave The Pedophocracy

33 Huysman, J.K. Irwin, Robert (ed..) La-Bas: Down There (Decadence from Dedalus)

MK-ULTRA:

34 https://etd.ohiolink.edu/!etd.send_file?accession=ohiou1406818924&disposition=inline

35 https://www.cbsnews.com/news/monster-study-still-stings/

36 Estabrooks, G.H., Ph.D Hypnosis Comes of Age,

37 Bain, Donald, The Control of Candy Jones, Chicago: Playboy Press (1976)

38 Ross, Colin A. The CIA Doctors: Human Rights Violations by American Psychiatrists, Manitou Communications (2006)

39 https://www.cia.gov/library/center-for-the-study-of-intelligence/csi-publications/csi-studies/studies/vol-58-no-3/operation-paperclip-the-secret-intelligence-program-to-bring-nazi-scientists-to-america.html

40 Delgado MD, Jose, Physical Control of the Mind: Toward a Psychocivilized Society,

41 http://www.pactsntl.org/assets/pcotmbydrjosed.pdf

42.. https://www.counterpunch.org/2017/11/17/the-cias-house-of-horrors-the-abominable-dr-gottlieb/ 43. (The CIA's House of Horrors: The Abominable Dr. Gottlieb)

44 Truthout, H.P. Albarelli & Jeffrey S. Kaye, 2010; The Hidden Tragedy of the CIA's Experiments on Children

45 https://www.nytimes.com/1977/08/02/archives/private-institutions-used-in-cia-effort-to-control-behavior-25year.html

46 NYT, Private Institutions Used in Cal Effort to Control Behavior, 1977 Drugs, sex, cybernetics and the Josiah Macy Foundation, Michael Minnicino, Executive Intelligence Review 1999

47 Virtual Government: CIA Mind Control Operations in America, Alex Constantine, 1997

48 The CIA and the Cult of Intelligence, Victor Marchetti & John Marks 1974

49 Chief, MKULTRA Task Force, CIA-RDP86-00100080003-9

50. Kinzer, Stephen, Poisoner-In-Chief,

51. https://www.mcgilltribune.com/mind-control-mcgill-mk-ultra/ The McGill Tribune, Declassified: 52. Mind Control at McGill Julie Vanderperre

52 https://nypost.com/2007/10/01/hillarys-30000-fans-are-her-cult-following/

51 http://disinfo.com/2015/09/leonard-cohens-secret-life-mkultra-cultural-engineering/

52 https://www.buddhistdoor.net/news/office-of-his-holiness-the-dalai-lama-issues-clarification-over-report-of-controversial-donation

False Memory Syndrome Foundation:

53 https://www.theatlantic.com/magazine/archive/2000/06/harvard-and-the-making-of-the-unabomber/378239/

54 nhttps://www.psychologytoday.com/sg/blog/impromptu-man/201205/harvards-experiment-the-unabomber-class-62

55 Aberration in the Heartland of the Real: The Secret Lives of Timothy McVeigh, Dr. Wendy S. Painting

56 Psychic Dictatorship in the USA, Alex Constantine (Feral House, 1995).

57 https://www.freedommag.org/english/la/issue02/page12.htm A clockwork orange career 61. https://theintercept.com/2019/11/24/cia-mkultra-louis-jolyon-west/

58 Inside the Archive of an LSD Researcher With Ties to the CIA's MKULTRA Mind Control Project, Intercept, Tom O'Neill, Dan Piepenbring, 2019

59 Toronto Star, 1996 Incest: Stop the Nonsense and Get to the Difficult Truth

60 https://madison.com/ct/news/local/crime_and_courts/blog/crime-and-courts-rethinking-the-false-memory-controversy/article_868cd71e-66ae-11e0-a171-001cc4c03286.html Rethinking the False Memory Controversy, Stephen Elbow

61 PBS Frontline, Divided Memories

62 https://www.tandfonline.com/doi/abs/10.1080/15379418.2019.1590285 Lost-in-the-mall: False memory or false defense, Ruth A. Blizzard & Morgan Shaw Journal of Child Custody

63 Applying Research to Parenting and Assessment Practice and Policies Volume 16, 2019 - Issue 1: Special Issue Part I: Misperceptions and Misapplications of Research in Family Law Cases: Myths of "Parental Alienation Syndrome" and Implanted False Memories, Guest Editor: Morgan Shaw Paul and Shirley Eberle: A Strange Pair of Experts , Ms Magazine 1988

64 McCarther, G. (2009, September 16). Psychiatrist admits inappropriate sexual relationship with patient. Retrieved from: https://www.news.com.au/news/doctor-admits-affair-wrong/news-story/2b8a6f303fa31e259000e4808f7022e2?sv=12e1f0d4921cf87a18278f757f64509f

65 Salter, A. (1998) "Confessions of a whistle blower: Lessons learned. Ethics and Behavior. 8(2), 115–124]

66 Andrews, B. & Brewin, C.R. (2017). False Memories and Free Speech: Is Scientific Debate Being Suppressed? Applied Cognitive Psychology, 31: 45–49. DOI: 10.1002/acp.3285

67. Becker-Blease, K. & Freyd, J.J. (2017). Additional Questions about the Applicability of "False Memory" Research, Applied Cognitive Psychology, 31: 34-36. DOI: 10.1002/acp.3266

68. O'Morain, P. "Irish Group Is Linked To Opponents of Child Abuse Programmes In US", Irish Times, 25 June 1996

69 https://news.isst-d.org/the-rise-and-fall-of-the-false-memory-syndrome-foundation/

70 https://finance.yahoo.com/news/survivors-celebrate-end-false-memory-223131484.html

71 Survivors Celebrate the End of the False Memory Syndrome Foundation After 27 Years Renee Fabian

72 Andrews, B. & Brewin, C.R. (2017). False Memories and Free Speech: Is Scientific Debate Being Suppressed? Applied Cognitive Psychology, 31: 45–49. DOI: 10.1002/acp.3285

73 Becker-Blease, K. & Freyd, J.J. (2017). Additional Questions about the Applicability of "False Memory" Research, Applied Cognitive Psychology, 31: 34-36. DOI: 10.1002/acp.3266

74 Brewin, C.R. & Andrews, B. (2017). Creating Memories for False Autobiographical Events in Childhood: A Systematic Review, Applied Cognitive Psychology, 31: 2–23. DOI: 10.1002/acp.3220

75 Freyd, J. & Birrell, P. (2013). Blind to Betrayal: Why we fool ourselves we aren't being fooled. John Wiley & Sons, Inc., Hoboken, New Jersey

76 Harrison, D. & Butcher, S. (2007, February 3). The shrink, his wife, a pistol and the ex, The Age. https://www.theage.com.au/national/the-shrink-his-wife-a-pistol-and-the-ex-20070203-ge450j.html

77 https://finance.yahoo.com/news/survivors-celebrate-end-false-memory-223131484.html

78 Survivors Celebrate the End of the False Memory Syndrome Foundation After 27 Years Renee Fabian

79 Andrews, B. & Brewin, C.R. (2017). False Memories and Free Speech: Is Scientific Debate Being Suppressed? Applied Cognitive Psychology, 31: 45–49. DOI: 10.1002/acp.3285

80 Becker-Blease, K. & Freyd, J.J. (2017). Additional Questions about the Applicability of "False Memory" Research, Applied Cognitive Psychology, 31: 34-36. DOI: 10.1002/acp.3266

81 Brewin, C.R. & Andrews, B. (2017). Creating Memories for False Autobiographical Events in Childhood: A Systematic Review, Applied Cognitive Psychology, 31: 2–23. DOI: 10.1002/acp.3220 Emery, E. and R. Flack "Plan would overhaul child abuse reporting / Lawmaker seeks greater protection for parents", Colorado Springs Gazette Telegraph Dvorchak, R (1992-08-22). "Custody Fights Use Sex Charge as Weapon". The Arizona Republic.

82 McCarther, G. (2009, September 16). Psychiatrist admits inappropriate sexual relationship with patient. https://www.news.com.au/news/doctor-admits-affair-wrong/news-story/2b8a6f303fa31e259000e4808f7022e2?sv=12e1f0d4921cf87a18278f757f64509f

83 Meinert, D. "Two-thirds of all child-abuse reports groundless, says study", San Diego Union-Tribune, 1985

84 Middleton, W. (2013) Parent–Child Incest that Extends into Adulthood: A Survey of International Press Reports, 2007–2011, Journal of Trauma & Dissociation, 14:2, 184-197, DOI: 10.1080/15299732.2013.724341

85 Salter, A. (1998) "Confessions of a whistle blower: Lessons learned. Ethics and Behavior. 8(2), 115–124]

Abuse of the Cloth:

86 https://www.smh.com.au/national/nsw/what-are-you-planning-to-say-pope-quizzed-whistleblower-priest-book-claims-20200819-p55n45.html

87 https://www.marketwatch.com/story/new-wave-of-sexual-abuse-lawsuits-could-cost-catholic-church-over-4-billion-2019-12-02

88 https://time.com/5762352/woman-sues-mormon-church-husband-child-sexual-abuse/

89 MormonLeaks, https://mormonleaks.io/

90 Vice News tonight Ep 535, MormonLeaks

91 https://avalaw.com/sexual-abuse/abused-in-mormonism/

92 https://abcnews.go.com/US/families-speak-church-jesus-christ-day-saints-sex/story?id=63690802https://www.vice.com/en_us/article/d3n73w/duty-to-report-the-mormon-church-has-been-accused-of-using-a-victims-hotline-to-hide-sexual-abuse-claims

93 https://kutv.com/news/local/mormonleaks-leaked-document-sheds-light-on-lds-churchs-handling-of-seven-sex-abuse-cases

94 https://record.adventistchurch.com/2019/05/16/healing-the-wounds-of-childhood-sexual-abuse/

95 https://www.bbc.com/news/uk-51006771

96 A&E Cults & Extreme Belief

97 https://www.nytimes.com/2009/10/14/nyregion/14abuse.html

98 https://www.childabuseroyalcommission.gov.au/narratives/meredith-annes-story

99 https://www.nytimes.com/2012/05/10/nyregion/ultra-orthodox-jews-shun-their-own-for-reporting-child-sexual-abuse.html

100 https://www.cjnews.com/news/health/child-sexual-abuse-in-community-rampant-audience-told

101 https://www.cjnews.com/news/health/child-sexual-abuse-in-community-rampant-audience-told

102 Ruth Wangerin, The Children of God: A Make-Believe Revolution?

103 https://www.livescience.com/16672-moammar-gadhafi-strange-behavior.html

104 https://www.livescience.com/coronavirus-superspreader-south-korea-church.html

105 Salvatore A. Pelle (August 1974). "Hawaii 1974: Baháí International youth conference". Baháí News. pp. 11–17. Retrieved Jan 19, 2015. https://www.jpost.com/middle-east/top-iranian-mp-bahai-are-mossad-and-cia-spies-341857

107 Lynch, Dalva, and Paul Carden (1990). "Inside the 'Heavenly Elite': The Children of God Today.". Christian Research Journal,

108 https://www.sfgate.com/news/article/Deaths-in-the-Family-Common-thread-of-sexual-2702662.php

109 https://www.theguardian.com/world/2017/mar/11/children-of-god-church-sex-cult-texas-mexico-fbi

110 The Children of God Cult, AKA The Family, Sam Ajemian

111 https://www.cesnur.org/testi/TheFamily/australia.htm

112 CESNUR, Center for Studies on New Religions, The Children of God/The Family in Court: A Documentary Legal History by Massimo Introvigne

113 https://blavatskytheosophy.com/the-unavoidable-facts-about-c-w-leadbeater/

114 Jiddu Krishnamurti: World Philosopher (1895-1986) : His Life and Thoughts By C. V. Williams

115 https://www.independent.co.uk/arts-entertainment/books/features/julian-assange-we-just-kept-moving-2359423.html

116 https://www.washingtonpost.com/wp-srv/national/longterm/cult/children_of_god/child1.htm

117 'The Family' and Final Harvest By Gustav Niebuhr, Washington Post Wednesday, June 2, 1993 (6 weeks after Waco)

118 CounterPunch, PARIAH, Scapegoats and Shunning

120. https://web.archive.org/web/20121105091411/http://www.highbeam.com/doc/15953847.html

December 16, 1994 | Goldston, Linda

121 Chicago Tribune https://archive.fo/VjncS

122 https://www.washingtonpost.com/archive/politics/1994/12/17/sex-abuse-allegations-fell-health-advocate/fc3bfe4b-14e3-45d8-823d-1c83b483e32f/

123 http://healthwrights.org/

https://www.theguardian.com/global-development/2018/feb/13/unicef-admits-failings-with-child-victims-of-alleged-sex-abuse-by-peacekeepers
124.https://www.hrw.org/news/2020/01/11/un-peacekeeping-has-sexual-abuse-problem

125. https://web.archive.org/web/20060822153007/http://politicsofhealth.org/

126 James Hunter MSW (2008) The Political Use and Abuse of the "Pedophile", Journal of Homosexuality, 55:3, 350-387, DOI: 10.1080/00918360802345073

SATANIC PANIC:

127 https://datacide-magazine.com/just-say-non-nazism-narcissism-and-boyd-rice/

128 https://www.nwprogressive.org/weblog/2020/08/instructive-bad-reading-part-four-dissecting-fascism-with-the-help-of-might-is-right.html

129 Aleister Crowley, "The Rights of Man" Liber AL XVII

130 CBC "What was the Satanic Panic"

131 NYT Retro-Report Dungeons and Dragons and the Satanic Panic

132 Lisa Bryn Rundle, Uncover the Satanic Panic

133 NYT Retro-Report "McMartin Preschool: Anatomy of a Panic"

134 Child Abuse at the Presidio: The parents' agony, the army's coverup, the prosecution's failure, San Jose Mercury, 1988

135 McMartin Preschool Revisited, Alex Constantine

FINDERS:

136 Dave McGowan, Programmed to Kill

137 Lanning, Kenneth "Satanic, Occult and Ritualistic Crime: A Law Enforcement Perspective" (Jun. 1989):

138 http://www.skeptictank.org/files/mys3/lanning.htm

139 https://www.washingtonpost.com/archive/politics/1987/02/07/officials-describe-cult-rituals-in-child-abuse-case/11f05df1-48e0-41f7-b46d-249c0bd2bc39/

140 FBI records: Vault, The Finders: https://vault.fbi.gov/the-finders

141 https://theduran.com/bombshell-debbie-wasserman-schultzs-it-specialist-subscribed-to-pedophile-centric-youtube-channels/

142 UPI, Communes back in the Spotlight; NEWLN: Today's communes blend '80s practicality with '60s idealism

143 3/2/98 Sun-Sentinel COMMUNES MIX '60S IDEALS, '80S REALITY - Sun Sentinel

144 The Finders and Patch Adams, Kenn Thomas, Tue, 22 Dec 1998

145 https://infidels.org/kiosk/article/a-freethinkers-haven-grows-inculpeper-257.html Kristin K. Nauth 2003

146 http://oregonlive.online/topic/jon-robberson-a-satanic-pedophile-ring-blackmailed-robin-williams-into-making/

FRANKLIN SCANDAL:

147 Nick Bryant, The Franklin Scandal: A Story of Powerbrokers, Child Abuse and Betrayal

148 https://en.wikipedia.org/wiki/Talk%3AFranklin_child_prostitution_ring_all egations%2FArchive_4#New_discussion_of_Bryant

149 Vanity Fair, Joe Pompeo Decoding Jeffrey Epstein's Star-Studded Black Book

https://www.vanityfair.com/news/2019/07/jeffrey-epstein-black-book-nick-bryant

150 (https://news.isst-d.org/an-interview-with-nick-bryant-part-i-the-franklin-scandal/)
https://www.niemanlab.org/2019/07/by-running-unwitting-pr-for-jeffrey-epstein-forbes-shows-the-risks-of-a-news-outlet-thinking-like-a-tech-platform/

151 U.S. News & World Report, Through a glass very darkly: Cops, spies and a very odd investigation 1993

152 Franklin Cover-Up John W. DeCamp

153 Who Took Johnny, David Bellinson, Suki Hawley, Michael Galinsky (2014 documentary)

154 WGNtv Chicago, Was John Wayne Gacy connected to a human trafficking ring? https://wgntv.com/news/cover-story/what-really-happened-to-michael-marino-investigation-begins/

155 CIA as organized Crime, Douglas Valentine

156 William Colby, man of contradictions found dead, AP news 1996

157 The Man Nobody Knew, Carl Colby documentary

158 Political Figures Linked to Male Prostitution Ring, AP news, 1989

159 Conspiracy of Silence, Discovery Channel

Jon Benet Ramsey:

160 Presumed Guilty: An investigation of the Jon Benet Ramsey Case, Singular, Stephen

161 https://decider.com/2019/10/14/kim-kardashian-oj-simpson-verdict-celebration/

162 Shocking Confession From the Jail Cell of Child Molester Gary Oliva. Star Magazine, January 2018

163 Who Killed Jon Benet Ramsey? Cyril Wecht

164 Stage: 'Hey, Rube' Tells of Ritual Killing, New York Times 1978

SAFE SCHOOLS:

165 https://www.ed.gov/about/offices/list/osdfs/index.html

166 "Why do we need an age of consent at all" https://youtu.be/5ZMHNMTzfeQ (Gary Dowsett lecture 2013)

167 https://www.dailymail.co.uk/news/article-3494915/George-Christensen-labels-academic-Gary-Dowsett-pedophilia-advocate-controversial-Safe-Schools-anti-bullying-program.html

168 https://web.archive.org/web/20180818212945/https://unsafeschools.org/the-australian-safe-schools-program-la-trobe-university/

169 Gay Information, Issue 11 "Boiled Lollies and Bandaids: Gay Men and Kids"

170 Queerty "mostly awesome gay activist" Harry Hay

171 (https://www.nambla.org/hay2002.htm)

172 (http://archive.md/a0eou)

173 Queerty, "Smear Campaigns: Kevin Jennings Supported a Gay Activist Who Once Supported NAMBLA. So He's a Pedophile?

174 Daily Beast, Hannity's Gay Target

175 Media Matters, https://www.mediamatters.org/red-state/months-after-its-been-debunked-redstate-casually-pushes-smear-kevin-jennings-pedophile

176 CBC, 2015 Benjamin Levin, https://www.cbc.ca/news/canada/manitoba/benjamin-levin-pleads-guilty-to-3-child-pornography-related-charges-1.2979621

177 Toronto Sun, Levin https://torontosun.com/2017/10/07/ex-deputy-education-minister-jailed-for-child-porn-charges-out-on-parole

United Kingdom:

178 Nudge and Wink: https://www.youtube.com/watch?v=XeB9ZxffQAE

179 Piers Morgan Live, 2015 Johnny Lydon

180 https://www.dailymail.co.uk/news/article-7973129/Polices-9m-probe-Operation-Hydrant-uncovers-hidden-child-abuse-epidemic-1970s-1980s.html

181 https://www.bbc.com/news/uk-28194271

https://www.bbc.com/news/uk-34801011

182 https://www.theguardian.com/politics/2014/mar/02/how-paedophiles-infiltrated-the-left-harriet-harman-patricia-hewitt

183 Savile and Andrew, https://www.thetimes.co.uk/article/deep-cover-jimmy-savile-fixed-it-for-warring-royals-cfrjjrptd86

184 https://www.bbc.com/news/uk-34801011

185 ITV, Exposure 2012 Jimmy Savile

186 BBC, Louis Theroux Savile

187 https://www.nspcc.org.uk/globalassets/documents/research-reports/yewtree-report-giving-victims-voice-jimmy-savile.pdf

188 https://www.theguardian.com/tv-and-radio/2017/jan/30/brass-eye-at-20-still-chris-morris-at-his-hysterical-gobsmacking-best

189 https://www.iicsa.org.uk/

190 somersetlive.co.uk/news/somerset-news/historic-abuse-sherborne-prep-council-1435620

191 https://policy.ciob.org/wp-content/uploads/2018/05/Construction-and-the-Modern-Slavery-Act-Tackling-Exploitation-in-the-UK-May-2018.pdf

192 https://www.theweek.co.uk/uk-news/62397/councillors-and-police-had-sex-with-rotherham-abuse-victims

193 thetimes.co.uk/article/child-slave-gangs-go-free-as-police-fail-to-investigate-sgjs8n2qc

194. hhttp://archive.rotherham.gov.uk/jsna/download/downloads/id/139/rotherham_demographic_profile_2017-18.pdf

195 https://www.independent.co.uk/news/uk/home-news/grooming-child-sex-abuse-exploitation-rotherham-rochdale-police-a9215261.html

196 https://www.telegraph.co.uk/women/life/tolerant-nation-time-shamed-grooming-gangs-prey-girls/201.
https://www.huffpost.com/entry/its-dj-vu-for-dyncorp-all_b_792394?guccounter=1

197 https://www.theguardian.com/uk-news/2019/oct/24/child-abuse-st-benedicts-school-ealing-abbey-iicsa-report

198 Ealing Abbey: Paedophiles acted 'like the mafia' 2019

Pop Culture & Pedophilia:

199 https://washingtonlife.com/tag/biljana-djurdjevic/ CBS News, Ben Swann investigates Pizzagate https://www.youtube.com/watch?v=KqCbMs5HzDo&list=LLSOrtA0leGHG5JfkHNq8SRQ&index=326

200 https://www.youtube.com/watch?v=4NLydwpvtus

201 Hollywood Babylon, Kenneth Anger

202 Pederastic Park, Adam Parfrey, https://feralhouse.com/wp/wp-content/uploads/2011/09/46188171-Pederastic-Park-Adam-Parfrey-on-Steven-Spielberg.pdf

203 conversation with Adam Parfrey

204 Answer Me! Jim Goad

205 ChickenHawk: Men who love boys, Adi Sideman 1994

206 https://www.worldcat.org/title/paedo-alert-news-a-magazine-about-boy-love/oclc/723967104

207 NAMBLA: Out of the Movement's Bounds, Richard J. Rosendall

208 https://www.lambdaliterary.org/tag/nambla/

209 Group Promoting man-boy love is the focus of police inquiry, New York Times, 1983

210 https://www.mirror.co.uk/tv/tv-news/hannah-montanas-dark-side-ruined-21746626

211 https://www.insider.com/bella-thorne-childhood-sexual-abuse-poetry-book-2019-7

212 https://www.theverge.com/culture/2017/11/21/16685874/kids-youtube-video-elsagate-creepiness-psychology

213 https://medium.com/@geoffgolberg/being-targeted-by-periscope-for-exposing-the-truth-22b63d0c351d

https://abcnews.go.com/Entertainment/story?id=4932313&page=1

215 James Bridle, https://medium.com/@jamesbridle/something-is-wrong-on-the-internet-c39c471271d2
https://ew.com/movies/corey-feldman-accuses-charlie-sheen-abuse-corey-haim-my-truth-documentary/
https://www.usmagazine.com/entertainment/pictures/zoey-101-cast-reunites-without-jamie-lynn-spears-pics/

The Jeffrey Epstein Affair:

216 https://www.nytimes.com/2019/11/26/business/jeffrey-epstein-charity.html

https://www.washingtonpost.com/politics/council-on-foreign-relations-another-beneficiary-of-epstein-largesse-grapples-with-how-to-handle-his-donations/2019/09/10/1d5630e2-d324-11e9-86ac-0f250cc91758_story.html

217 https://www.theguardian.com/us-news/2019/aug/22/the-murky-life-and-death-of-robert-maxwell-and-how-it-shaped-his-daughter-ghislaine

218 https://www.natlawreview.com/article/art-and-money-laundering#:~:text=Art%20is%20an%20attractive%20vehicle,as%20well%20as%20extremely%20high.&text=Once%20inside%20the%20freeport%2C%20the,and%20anonymously%20to%20other%20buyers.

219 https://www.insider.com/ghislaine-maxwell-jeffrey-epstein-alleged-madame-2019-7#after-fleeing-to-new-york-maxwell-rubbed-elbows-with-some-of-the-citys-highfliers-including-the-real-estate-developer-donald-trump-2

https://www.gq-magazine.co.uk/culture/article/jeffrey-epstein-filthy-rich-review-netflix

220 https://www.npr.org/2019/08/22/753390385/a-dead-cat-a-lawyers-call-and-a-5-figure-donation-how-media-fell-short-on-epstei

221 https://www.businessinsider.com/ghislaine-maxwell-attended-kleiner-perkins-vc-party-alleges-ellen-pao-2020-7

222 https://pagesix.com/2017/10/04/jeffrey-epstein-paid-5-5m-to-settle-lawsuits/?_ga=2.59154541.1742053680.1506923348-1066152109.1506336895

223 https://www.sun-sentinel.com/news/fl-palm-epstein-mayocol-b020515-20150204-column.html

224 http://www.topix.com/forum/city/delray-beach-fl/TEPHA5A0VGN4QACGQ/hafele-appointed-to-circuit-judgeship

225 https://www.palmbeachpost.com/news/crime--law/ponzi-schemer-rothstein-wooing-politicians-including-crist-and-mccain-key-success/Iz51TrOFgrvAxo5UyAXN5O/

DIGITAL PLAYGROUND:

225 https://www.bbc.com/news/blogs-trending-42060357

226 https://www.independent.co.uk/news/business/news/youtube-adverts-paedophiles-children-videos-access-comments-a8073181.html

227 https://variety.com/2017/digital/news/youtube-toy-freaks-channel-terminated-1202617834/#article-comments

228 https://www.buzzfeednews.com/article/charliewarzel/youtube-tween-channel-owner-arrested-for-molesting

229 https://www.tubefilter.com/2019/03/13/youtube-sevenawesomekids-ian-rylett-terminated/

230 https://www.newsweek.com/top-5-youtube-scandals-2019-shane-dawson-fantastic-adventures-ace-family-more-1370626

231 https://filmdaily.co/news/shane-dawson-jokes/

232 https://vt.co/news/entertainment-news/family-youtuber-denies-allegations-after-16-year-old-fan-accuses-him-of-trying-to-get-her-alone

233 On Youtube's Digital Playground, an Open Gate for Pedophiles, 2019 New York Times

234 NCOSE Dirty Dozen, endsexualexploitation.org/project-tax/youtube/

235 https://steemit.com/exposingexploitation/@aagabriel/alice-day-part-1-academia-belankazar-child-modelling-in-venezuela

236 https://www.theverge.com/2019/2/19/18229938/youtube-child-exploitation-recommendation-algorithm-predators

237 https://www.justice.gov/usao-md/pr/essex-man-sentenced-17-years-federal-prison-sexual-exploitation-child-produce-child

238 https://www.justice.gov/usao-ednc/pr/raleigh-man-who-convicted-sex-offender-sentenced-20-years-receipt-child-pornography

239 https://www.forbes.com/sites/thomasbrewster/2017/08/03/kik-has-a-massive-child-abuse-problem/#7987836d1a14

240. Wildly Popular App Kik Offers Teenagers, and Predators, Anonymity, New York Times, 2016

241 https://youtu.be/ZYmwGoqtgx0

242 https://www.kqed.org/mindshift/56339/when-it-comes-to-screens-kids-need-a-guide-not-a-disciplinarian

243 https://www.justice.gov/usao-mdla/pr/denham-springs-man-sentenced-25-years-federal-prison-child-pornography-convictions

244 Facebook asked users if pedophiles should be able to ask kids for 'sexual pictures' USA Today

245 https://deadline.com/2020/08/hasbro-pull-trolls-world-tour-doll-1203006592/

246 https://www.indiewire.com/2018/05/show-dogs-controversy-private-parts-1201967544/

247 https://www.irishpost.com/news/controversial-book-claims-elvis-presley-paedophile-preyed-underage-girls-166753

248 https://www.kqed.org/arts/13867962/not-just-joker-americas-been-ignoring-gary-glitters-pedophilia-for-years

249 Kimball, Roger The perversions of M. Foucault

250 Miller, James On The Passion of Michel Foucault

251 https://arcdigital.media/the-pedophile-apologist-40ee80bf5d58 Justin Lee

252 https://www.latimes.com/world-nation/story/2020-02-21/french-writer-gabriel-matzneff-pedophile

253. A Witchhunt Foiled: The FBI vs. NAMBLA (New York: NAMBLA, 1985)

254 https://www.forbes.com/sites/denizcam/2019/06/14/how-a-du-pont-heir-avoided-jail-time-for-a-heinous-crime/#23d0f40c29db

255 https://www.cs.cmu.edu/~dst/Library/Shelf/miller/bfm18.htm

256. https://eastmesa.macaronikid.com/articles/5b017dc3700a6450421ef1c2

257 https://www.latimes.com/archives/la-xpm-2002-jun-23-ca-lucas23-story.html

258 http://celebrityinsider.org/some-question-abcs-and-disneys-willingness-to-work-with-registered-sex-offenders-and-pedophiles-after-immediately-canceling-roseanne-152501/

259 Lucas, Michael P. "Groomed to Be All That" (2002) https://www.latimes.com/archives/la-xpm-2002-jun-23-ca-lucas23-story.html

260 https://articles.latimes.com/1995-10-31/entertainment/ca-63118_1_victor-salva

261 https://www.imdb.com/name/nm0412639/

263 https://www.homefacts.com/offender-detail/CA27402111G1648/Joel-Edward-Iwataki.html

264 https://www.nbcmiami.com/news/local/mom-fights-to-ban-child-sex-dolls-after-daughters-likeness-was-used-for-one/2287435/

265 https://culteducation.com/group/977-hosanna-church/9842-lamonica-convicted-of-raping-two-sons.html

266 https://www.dailymail.co.uk/news/article-3976078/Radio-presenter-accused-British-photographer-David-Hamilton-child-rape-left-devastated-cowardly-suicide-justice-won-t-able-work.html

267 https://www.theatlantic.com/international/archive/2018/03/frances-existential-crisis-over-sexual-harassment-laws/550700/

268 https://www.seniorsnews.com.au/news/australian-celebrity-paedophile-ring-revealed/3438196/

269 https://www.dailymail.co.uk/news/article-3976078/Radio-presenter-accused-British-photographer-David-Hamilton-child-rape-left-devastated-cowardly-suicide-justice-won-t-able-work.html

270 https://www.walmart.com/ip/Bilitis/179569402

271 https://www.walmart.com/ip/A-Summer-in-Saint-Tropez-DVD/55453701

272 https://childusa.org/member-docs/Secrecy%20Rules%20Against%20Scandal%20by%20Marci%20Hamilton%20.pdf

273 https://vigilantcitizen.com/latestnews/something-is-terribly-wrong-with-the-childrens-clothing-line-caroline-bosmans/

274 https://www.medscape.com/viewarticle/887592

275 https://www.newstatesman.com/science-tech/internet/2018/08/catch-child-predator-youtube-s-latest-morally-dubious-trend

276 https://www.nbcnews.com/news/us-news/he-lures-alleged-child-predators-shames-them-facebook-now-one-n953856?cid=sm_npd_nn_tw_ma

277 https://knowyourmeme.com/memes/the-ratio

278 https://www.mirror.co.uk/news/uk-news/man-47-kills-himself-two-13048793

279 https://www.telegraph.co.uk/news/2019/09/10/one-five-children-groomed-online-aged-12-nspcc-figures-reveal/

280 https://www.bbc.com/news/uk-47410520

281 https://www.euronews.com/2020/05/29/facebook-apps-used-in-at-least-a-third-of-child-grooming-cases-says-uk-children-s-charity

282 https://www.bbc.com/news/uk-47410520

Epilogue

283 https://www.theguardian.com/film/2020/sep/14/cuties-review-netflixs-controversial-child-exploitation-film-is-bold-flawed-and-misunderstood

284 https://time.com/5886184/cuties-netflix-maimouna-doucoure/

285 https://www.distractify.com/p/imdb-cuties-warning

286 https://www.npr.org/2020/09/06/909753465/cuties-calls-out-the-hypersexualization-of-young-girls-and-gets-criticized

287 https://wtop.com/entertainment/2020/08/netflix-makes-changes-to-cuties-following-petition/

288. https://www.reddit.com/r/IAmA/comments/abli1b/im_max_karson_i_was_quite_publicly_arrested_in/

289 https://www.upi.com/Archives/1981/11/11/Judge-scolds-Brooke-Shields-mother-for-exploiting-daughter/9143374302800/

290 https://www.nytimes.com/1983/03/30/nyregion/brooke-shields-loses-court-case.html

Printed in Great Britain
by Amazon